TERENCE

THE MOTHER-IN-LAW

Socrui Meae

TERENCE

The Mother in Law

SOSTRATA MULIER   PAMPHILUS ADULESCENS   LACHES SENEX

edited with translation, introduction and commentary
by

S. IRELAND

British Library Cataloguing in Publication Data
Terence *186 or 5 B.C. - 160 B.C.*
    Mother-in-Law. - (Classical Texts, ISSN 0953-7961)
    1. Drama in Latin, to ca 500 - Latin-English parallel text
    I. Title II. Ireland, S. III. Series

ISBN 0 85668 373 6 cloth
ISBN 0 85668 374 4 limp

Printed and bound by CPI Group (UK) Ltd, Croydon CR0 4YY

CONTENTS

PREFACE

Terence's *The Mother-in-Law* is not a funny play. To describe it as a comedy at all strains the meaning of the word in all its modern connotations; nor does it seem to have impressed itself upon its ancient audiences, for its first two attempted presentations failed in the face of what at the time were more congenial forms of entertainment. In many respects, however, it is this very lack of conventional humour that first attracted me to it, since it is clear that Terence was deliberately attempting to break new ground with his play, tantalising his audiences with ostensibly blatant rejection of standard comic technique, developing a theme that contained more than a hint of potential tragedy, emphasising dramatic tension and suspense, and only rescuing the obligatory happy ending in the closing lines of the action.

In producing this edition I have attempted to provide the reader with an English version of the Latin that is readable while at the same time close enough to the original to make comparison of the two a less than daunting proposition. The Notes to the Translation in turn are aimed at explaining the main dramatic developments that take place in the action and to provide some idea of the subtleties that Terence injected into his work. In their production I am, of course, indebted to those many commentators who have written on the play in the past. Only rarely, however, for reasons of space and the format of the series, have I been able to acknowledge the extent of my debt, though I hope that the Bibliography goes some way towards rectifying this. My thanks too must go to the publishers, Aris and Phillips, whose resolute patience cushioned the unavoidable interruptions in writing caused by an unscheduled change of university, and to their Editorial Advisor, Prof. M.M. Willcock, whose constantly available and sympathetic advice slimmed down an otherwise bloated volume to manageable proportions. I would also like to acknowledge a debt of gratitude to Dr. Rachel Parkins of Warwick University's Computing Services Centre who has guided me through the traumas of producing camera-ready copy with remarkable good humour. Finally, a special word of thanks to my wife, Helen, for being there with unfailing encouragement when problems seemed intractable and the way ahead strewn with boulders.

INTRODUCTION

THE LIFE AND CAREER OF TERENCE

By ancient tradition Publius Terentius Afer was a native of Carthage, raised as a slave in the household of the Roman Senator, Terentius Lucanus, who educated him and subsequently set him free. This we learn from the biography of the playwright composed by Suetonius in the second century A.D. and preserved in the fourth century commentary on the plays by Donatus (a translation is appended to the Penguin Terence). Ostensibly the biography is a rich source of factual information. In many respects, however, it is little more than a patchwork of supposition derived from earlier writers, whose disagreement over even the most basic of details suggests a heavy dependence upon what could be gleaned from the Production Notices attached to the plays, the prologues to the plays themselves, and ultimately imagination. That Terence was reared as a slave may indeed be true, but by the same token it may be little more than inference from the Afer ("African") element of his name, and thus no more valid than a literal interpretation of any name.

Similarly disputed is the date of Terence's birth. Some ancient writers placed it in the period before 201 B.C., the end of the Second Punic War; others made him a contemporary of Scipio Aemilianus, born in 185 B.C., while some manuscripts of Donatus suggest a date for Terence's birth c. 195 B.C. After the production of his final play, *The Brothers*, in 160 B.C. Terence disappears from history. Tradition held that he died while visiting or returning from Greece, where he had evidently gone to acquire fresh material for adaptation onto the Roman stage. Again, however, we find variation, not only in the reason for his departure from Rome, but also in the location of his death (at sea, Leucadia, Stymphalus) and its cause (shipwreck, illness, or grief at the loss of plays sent on ahead).

Details concerning the actual literary career of Terence provided by the Production Notices to the plays inspire greater confidence and suggest that the six plays which have come down to us constitute his total output. Discrepancies as to their order of composition and their dating certainly exist - largely as a result of attempts to reconcile the evidence the Notices give with that provided by the prologues and Donatus (see Marti[2] p.20ff.) - but the generally accepted order is:

Andria (The Woman from Andros) 166 B.C.
Hecyra (The Mother-in-Law) 1st failure 165 B.C.
Heautontimorumenos (The Self-Tormentor) 163 B.C.
Eunuchus (The Eunuch) 161 B.C.
Phormio 161 B.C.
Hecyra 2nd failure 160 B.C.
Adelphoe (The Brothers) 160 B.C.
Hecyra 3rd and successful production 160 B.C.

       As plays none is totally original. The drama of Terence, like that of Plautus before him, belongs to the genre of the *fabulae palliatae*, comedy in Greek dress (*pallium* or Greek cloak) adapted for Roman audiences from the productions of Greek New Comedy, the main exponents of which were Menander, Diphilus, and Philemon, all active in Athens over a hundred years before (see Sandbach[2], Brothers p.1ff.). Of Terence's six works four (*Andria, Heautontimorumenos, Eunuchus* and *Adelphoe*) were taken from Menander, the remaining two (*Hecyra* and *Phormio*) from Apollodorus of Carystus, himself much influenced by Menander. Terence displays a similar preference for particular religious festivals - the usual occasion for stage productions and other forms of entertainment in Rome (Duckworth[2] p.76ff.). Of the six plays four - *Andria, Hecyra* (first failure), *Heautontimorumenos* and *Eunuchus* - were staged at the *Ludi Megalenses*, held each year in April to honour Cybele, the Great Mother goddess of Asia Minor. The remainder were produced either at the *Ludi Romani* held annually in September (*Phormio* and perhaps the third presentation of *Hecyra*), or at the *Ludi Funebres*, funeral games, held in 160 B.C. to honour the dead Aemilius Paulus (*Adelphoe* and *Hecyra's* second failure).

       Though taken from Greek plays, the adaptations of Plautus and Terence were never mere translations. True, they retained the Greek flavour of setting, character types and ethos, but the very nature of the Roman audience and the appeal of native Italian comic forms demanded changes of emphasis, structure and style that are clear despite our inability to compare a single Roman play with its Greek original. So for instance, on the level of structure the extant plays of Menander are divided into five Acts by choral interludes unconnected with the action and inserted for predominantly historical reasons. As a result their contents have failed to survive. Within the Acts themselves some 80% of the text is set in spoken verse dialogue; the rest consists of longer metres delivered with musical accompaniment as a kind of 'recitative'. In producing their adaptations the Roman authors omitted the choral interludes altogether, creating in effect a single continuous flow of action. Plautus, however, did not forego the musical element of the Greek plays completely; rather, he transferred it to his own versions in the form of lyrics from the actors. Terence on the other hand retained almost exclusively the dialogue-recitative format of his originals, producing as a result a more homogeneous, but at the same time a far more restrained, form of drama (see further Commentary 39 n.).

The changes introduced by Terence, however, go further than the simple omission of Act divisions. The plays themselves indicate a conscious determination to move away from plot exposition by means of a prologue, such as is found in many of the works of Menander and Plautus, to a more natural technique based on the gradual revelation of information within the body of the action (cf. *Adelphoe* 22ff.). Only in response to external pressures was Terence forced to reintroduce a form of prologue, not for exposition, but with the novel purpose of countering the many problems that beset his work. In the case of *Hecyra*, with its unprecedented two prologues and their reference to three separate performances, these arose from the fickleness of his Roman audiences and their apparent preference for livelier forms of entertainment. In 165 B.C., for instance, the prospect of a tight-rope walker and the rumour of a boxing match caused an influx of new spectators into the theatre which effectively brought the production of his play to a premature halt. At the second presentation early in 160 the disaster was repeated, this time through the rumoured promise of a gladiatorial display (see further the Commentary on the Prologues). With the other plays the problems centre upon charges made by a figure Terence himself refers to as "a spiteful old poet" (*Andria* 6f., *Heautontimorumenos* 22) and whom Donatus identified as Luscius Lanuvinus (Garton p.41ff., Grimal). From the attempts at defence four main accusations emerge:

1. *Contaminatio*, spoiling the Greek originals by inserting into the Roman adaptation material derived from another Greek play (*Andria* 16, *Heautontimorumenos* 17f., see further Duckworth[2] p.61ff., Beare[2] p.96ff., 310ff., Goldberg p.91ff., Arnott[1] p.48ff.).
2. Plagiarism, taking material from another Latin play (*Eunuchus* 23ff., *Adelphoe* 6ff.) and thus breaking the convention which had evidently developed of not reworking a play or parts of a play already adapted for the Roman stage.
3. Receiving help in the composition of his plays from aristocratic friends (*Heautontimorumenos* 22ff., *Adelphoe* 15ff.). From this perhaps came the tradition of Terence's close association with the so-called Scipionic circle (see further Goldberg p.8ff.).
4. Feeble composition, a charge found at *Phormio* 5, suggesting that Terence's plays were light-weight productions unworthy of serious consideration. Significantly, it was Terence's "mild tone" (*sedatis motibus*) and "gentle writing" (*lenibus...scriptis*) that Cicero and Caesar were themselves later to regard as worthy of specific mention (see Goldberg p.180).

The fact that the source of our information concerning the charges is Terence himself has, of course, its own implications for any detailed understanding of them. Can we, for instance, be certain that Terence accurately reflected the nature of the charges made, or, faced with the almost insuperable problem of their refutation within the compass of a few lines of verse, did he simplify and obscure them almost beyond recognition? Was his tacit acceptance of some of the charges in fact a means of deflecting attention away from the true originality of the alterations made (Beare[3])? We shall never know, any more than we shall know if the rival attractions Terence claims beset *Hecyra* were the real source of that play's difficulties.

Within the history of Roman Comedy Terence stands as the younger of the two playwrights whose works have survived. Before him towers the prodigious figure of Plautus (c. 254-184 B.C.), a supreme exponent of robust humour and farce, who mingled together song and dance, the burlesque and the almost serious, ranging far and wide in his presentation of character and plot, and always ready to halt the flow of action and to stand convention on its head for the sake of a laugh. In him Roman Comedy saw the culmination of that unique blend of Greek New Comedy and native Italian wit that had been developing through writers like Naevius (c. 270-201 B.C.) since the presentation of the first *fabula palliata* at Rome by Livius Andronicus traditionally dated to 240 B.C. After Terence, in whose works commentators have often seen evidence of a conscious effort to transfer in full to the Roman stage the qualities of Menander - hence perhaps Caesar's tag "oh half-Menander" - New Comedy at Rome reverted to its older style, wearing out its stock formulations until it vanished as a living genre at the end of the second century B.C.

As a writer of *fabulae palliatae* Terence represents a unique experiment: an attempt to provide his audience with the unity and sophistication of Greek New Comedy while at the same time departing from much of its basic technique by demanding of that same audience a degree of attention to detail it was evidently not capable of giving. It cannot be without significance that ancient tradition holds *The Eunuch* to be the playwright's most popular play, whereas the sombre, almost tragic, tones of *The Mother-in-Law* could scarcely gain a hearing at all.

THE MOTHER-IN-LAW

Summary of the Plot

More than any other work by Terence *The Mother-in-Law* depends for its effect upon ignorance and misapprehension embracing both stage characters and audience alike until almost the very end of the play. A prime result of this is the enormous reliance placed upon supposition and inference, which time and again lead to conclusions that prove ultimately ill-founded.

The action opens with the appearance of two women, both of them professional types or 'courtesans', who make their living by providing female company for any man able to pay. Their topic of conversation, upon which the audience eavesdrops, is a visit to their friend Bacchis from whom one of them, Philotis, has just learned of the breakdown in the long-standing relationship between Bacchis and her lover Pamphilus as a result of his marriage. To Syra, Philotis' companion, the event merely demonstrates the innate unreliability of men, an unduly harsh verdict in Philotis' eyes, as a new character onstage soon confirms, Pamphilus' slave Parmeno. From the outset Parmeno's whole demeanour suggests he is the type of slave who might be expected to rescue his master from any predicament and provide a sympathetic and confidential ear for his innermost thoughts and emotions. From him Philotis learns that blame for the breach in relations must take two factors into account: first, that Pamphilus was an unwilling participant in his marriage; second, that the coolness which developed between the two lovers originated with Bacchis herself. It is as a result of her behaviour that Pamphilus was eventually induced to transfer his affections to his young wife, Philumena, whom he had regarded till then with thinly veiled hostility. No sooner had the transfer of emotion been effected, however, than Pamphilus was sent off to Imbros to collect an inheritance, leaving his wife at home with her mother-in-law. For a time all went well between the two, but gradually for some unspecified reason relations became strained to the point where Philumena returned to her parents' home and refused any further contact.

With the mystery of the girl's absence established, all three figures leave, and it is onto an empty stage that Pamphilus' parents emerge, his father Laches and Sostrata his mother. From the start it is clear that Laches blames his wife for the departure of their daughter-in-law, though in his ill-tempered outburst he seems more intent upon pouring scorn on Sostrata than upon reaching any objective understanding of the situation. Not that Sostrata can help in this; for apart from knowing she has done nothing to merit Philumena's dislike, she has no explanation for the girl's departure. To Laches on the other hand no explanation is necessary. In true 'old man' fashion he is more than content to let conventional prejudice against mothers-in-law bolster his predisposition to regard his wife as the cause of any mishap within his household.

The appearance at this point of Philumena's father, Phidippus, offers the prospect of getting to the bottom of the mystery. In the event, however, cross-questioning by Laches serves merely to increase confusion over the cause of Philumena's behaviour and to reveal Phidippus as totally incapable of controlling his womenfolk. In consequence the two old men leave, having achieved little except to convince Laches even more of his wife's culpability.

Onto the stage now come Parmeno and his young master Pamphilus, fresh back from Imbros and plunged into despair at the news of what has happened. Despite some weak attempts by the slave to relieve the darkness it is in fact Pamphilus who proves more accurate in his analysis of events, with himself the victim torn by conflicting loyalties in the supposed theme of enmity between his mother and his wife. At this, however, a new thread is injected into the situation by cries of pain coming from Philumena inside her parents' home. Pamphilus dashes indoors to discover the cause, while Parmeno, left onstage, can only dissuade Sostrata from following suit when she reappears from her own house in response to those same cries. Soon Pamphilus emerges again - stunned at what he has found but nevertheless able to deflect his mother's enquiries and to persuade her back indoors, while Parmeno is sent off to help the porters with the luggage. Thus left alone the young man pours out his tale of woe - a wife found in the throes of giving birth to a child that cannot possibly be his own, the result of pre-marital rape by an unknown assailant. Love for Philumena and an assurance from her mother Myrrina that the infant will be disposed of induce Pamphilus not to reveal the girl's disgrace, but her sullied state prevents him from regarding her ever again as his wife. The promise of silence given to Myrrina is immediately threatened, however, by the reappearance of Parmeno and his fellow slave Sosia - Parmeno, the only other member of Laches' household who will realise the child was not conceived in wedlock. No sooner is Parmeno disposed of - sent on a wild-goose chase - than an even greater threat presents itself with the return onstage of Laches and Phidippus, convinced as they are that the arrival of Pamphilus will automatically solve all difficulties. To counter their expectations Pamphilus is forced into resurrecting the theme of enmity between mother and wife, now though as his excuse for not taking Philumena back. To Laches and Phidippus the young man's attitude beggars comprehension, but before the matter can be taken further Pamphilus rushes from the stage and the two old men withdraw into their respective houses in varying states of annoyance.

At this point a mirror image of the earlier scene between Laches and Sostrata is brought before the audience, this time between Myrrina and Phidippus who has discovered the existence of the child and sees its concealment as evidence of his wife's continuing dislike for her son-in-law, a dislike engendered initially by his affair with Bacchis. For her part Myrrina is prepared to use any element of misapprehension in Phidippus' mind to avoid the truth, and by exercising her more forceful willpower she induces Phidippus to accept at least the possibility of her supposed dislike being justified. Once Phidippus is out of the way Myrrina is able to reveal more details of the rape - the fact that her daughter also lost a ring to her assailant - together with the implications for Pamphilus of the child being kept alive.

As Myrrina withdraws, out of Laches' house come Sostrata and Pamphilus, his earlier attempt to avoid further marital relations with Philumena by championing his mother's cause now radically undermined by Sostrata's own determination to reward her son's loyalty by retiring to the country. This she calculates will remove any ostensible reason for Philumena not returning to her husband, the one thing of course that Pamphilus does not want. Worse still is the intervention first of Laches, who accepts his wife's offer, and then of Phidippus, who not only shifts responsibility for the breakdown of the marriage away from Sostrata and onto Myrrina, but also further widens knowledge of the baby's existence. Faced with Pamphilus' less than enthusiastic reaction to the news of the child Laches finally loses his temper and interprets his son's continuing refusal to take Philumena back as no more than a pretext designed to disguise the real cause: a supposed resumption of the affair with Bacchis. Unable to counter his father's arguments for fear of an even worse truth, Pamphilus once again rushes from the stage leaving the two old men to determine upon a stern warning to Bacchis as the best course to pursue.

With Phidippus sent to arrange a nurse for the infant Laches confronts his son's former mistress. Impressed, however, by her assurances that there has been nothing between herself and Pamphilus since the marriage, he concludes that any prejudice Myrrina has against her son-in-law must be ill-founded and will disappear altogether once she too hears those same assurances. The reappearance of Phidippus at this point means that, for all his hostility towards Bacchis, he too is drawn into the latest projected course of action.

As all leave we see the return of a weary Parmeno, worn out by the errand his master had sent him on and soon confronted with another. This time it is Bacchis, fresh from Phidippus' house, who despatches him to find Pamphilus with the message that Myrrina has recognised the ring he gave her some time ago. Once alone onstage Bacchis is at long last able to clear up the mystery of the play: the ring, the spoils of rape, reveals Pamphilus as the father of the very child he earlier thought illegitimate, a fact that Pamphilus himself has clearly grasped by the time he returns with Parmeno to greet Bacchis as his saviour. Between them the two determine to restrict knowledge of the truth to those who need to know, which effectively rules out both old men and Parmeno, with whose constantly frustrated desire to penetrate the ignorance imposed upon him the play draws to its close.

Terentian Technique in the Play

Alone among Terence's plays *Hecyra* lacks a dual plot - the inclusion of a second love-intrigue. It is also remarkable for its seriousness and its essentially static nature, depicting as it does a situation in which characters are so isolated from one another by the circumstances in which they are caught up and by the fabrications they weave that monologue becomes an almost standard mode of expression (cf. Denzler p.134ff.). From this perhaps stems in · part the wide diversity of reaction the play has evoked from modern commentators: "the purest and most perfect example of classical high comedy" wrote Norwood (p.90); "of least merit" was Ashmore's verdict (p.33).

In essence the plot of *The Mother-in-Law* is centred not upon the usual theme of a young bachelor's love-escapade, such as forms the basis of the other plays, but upon the problems that endanger an already established marriage. In many ways, in fact, the play begins where many another comedy plot leaves off (Konstan p.133). The occurrence of a supposedly illegitimate birth poses of course an immediate threat to the whole foundation of the marriage in question. Social convention indeed demanded its termination through divorce and disgrace for the young bride, whose only 'crime' had been to fall victim to rape. In terms of comic technique the only escape from such a situation would be the discovery that the whole question of illegitimacy was no more than a red herring, that the child was actually the offspring of the young couple, though conceived in ignorance and outside wedlock, as for instance in Menander's *Epitrepontes* (*Arbitration*). By denying his audience total certainty of such an outcome, however, Terence immediately places greater emphasis upon genre expectations to mitigate the essentially tragic overtones of a situation in which the audience share with the characters on the stage the gradual revelation of details. That the play is classed as a comedy carries with it, of course, the natural expectation of a happy ending, but how this is to be achieved in the situation as presented becomes in itself a major source of interest. Certainly, a rational approach on the part of the audience within the context of comic convention could only have suggested that ultimately rapist and young husband would turn out to be one and the same. Yet on more than one occasion Terence ostensibly rejects or reverses what might otherwise have provided pointers to a predictable outcome. Myrrina's reference to the ring lost by her daughter in the course of the rape is a case in point, since it was normal New Comedy technique for the assailant to lose some article of his own by which he would later be identified, not his victim. The result in effect is a heightening of tension as the audience sees potential avenues of escape from disaster being closed one after another.

Suspense within *The Mother-in-Law* is founded largely upon the dilemma into which Pamphilus finds himself plunged on his return from Imbros. As the young husband faced with a child that is not his own and a wife disgraced by rape he is pulled in two directions: 1) his responsibility towards his family, which demands repudiation of Philumena, and 2) his attempts, born of love, to protect his wife from the implications of her state, while at the same time avoiding a resumption of marital relations. The dilemma deepens as those around him, ignorant of the true situation and of the motives which spur him to take the course he does, act - often for the noblest reasons - in ways that seem calculated to produce the very disaster Pamphilus wishes to avoid. Time and again he is forced into developing the theme of resentment as a means of defence, shifting responsibility - albeit understandably - onto those who do not deserve it. Significantly, when salvation does come, its source is not Pamphilus, whose efforts have simply ensnared him ever more tightly in his dilemma, but the two old men, who are largely responsible for the impasse, together with Bacchis, who emerges like a *deus ex machina* to unite what have so far been disparate factors into the necessary solution.

For audiences accustomed to the often blatant transparency of Plautine comedy the depth of misapprehension which Terence imposes upon those that viewed *The Mother-in-Law* must have come as no small dramatic shock. Though the playwright nowhere makes any overt reference to the problems arising from his novel technique, we cannot but wonder if the two abortive productions, first in 165, then in 160, were caused as much by the complex uncertainties of the action as by the extraneous interference of a tight-rope walker and rumours of boxing or gladiatorial contests upon which Terence chooses to concentrate. Certainly the unflattering picture of the audience given in the first prologue is highly suggestive of attention wandering from stage action which offered little in the way of conventional humour to other, more immediately appreciable forms of entertainment. As Goldberg observes p.168, it can hardly be a mere accident of scheduling that caused *The Mother-in-Law*'s second failure at the funeral games for Aemilius Paulus yet left *The Brothers* totally unscathed (contrast Gilula[5]).

TERENCE AND THE GREEK ORIGINAL

For all the attractiveness of *Hecyra*'s internal developments commentators have frequently preferred to concentrate their attention upon gauging and analysing the relationship between Terence's adaptation and the lost Greek original. To the cynic such an exercise cannot but appear a totally misguided, albeit congenial, squandering of effort, and he may well be forgiven for finding confirmation of his prejudice in the very disparate nature of the conclusions reached. At one extreme, for instance, stands the work of Kuiper, for whom the Terentian version represents such a radical reworking of the Apollodoran play that their common origin becomes at times hardly recognisable. At the other extreme are the arguments of Sewart[1] and Flickinger[2&3], who regard the changes introduced within the body of the action as minimal or unimportant.

Though it is lost, the fact that the Apollodoran play existed within a genre dominated by convention does allow a number of assumptions to be made concerning its structure and aims. At the same time references by Donatus to that same original provide an additional source of information, even if the importance and significance to be attached to the commentator's observations remain contentious. So for instance, the rediscovery this century of substantial sections of plays by Menander has confirmed for Greek New Comedy what had previously been suspected on the basis of Plautus' work - that the Greek plays placed great emphasis upon exposition of a plot's antecedents by means of a prologue, situated either at the very beginning of the action, as in the case of *Dyskolos* (*Old Cantankerous*), or after an initial scene had established the situation as known to the humans involved, as with *Aspis* (*Shield*, cf. Plautus' *Cistellaria* and *Miles Gloriosus*, Sandbach[1] p.20f.). It is in fact such a deferred prologue that Sewart[3] p.258f. cogently argues occurred in the Greek *Hecyra* following the departure of Parmeno at 197. Postponement to this point, after all, would introduce an element of economy into the drama, placing the emphasis for exposition squarely onto the slave's shoulders, only subsequently to be corrected - without the need for repetition - by a better informed source, as Tyche or Chance does in Menander's *Aspis*. It would also remove from Parmeno at an early stage that position of authoritative informant and confidant he has so far assumed, so that his subsequent interaction with Pamphilus could be seen as all the more misguided and amusing. One immediate result of employing the prologue as a means of exposition is concentration upon dramatic irony - when the audience knows more than the characters on the stage - as the major comic effect. That Apollodorus followed Menander in this, as apparently in so much else, is a generally accepted premise for any study of the Greek version. Such a prologue, delivered in all probability by some omniscient deity or personified abstraction who would automatically have possessed a greater understanding of the true situation, must have contained the real reason for Philumena's departure from her marital home and the identity of her assailant. On this after all depends the audience's ability to see through the misapprehensions that occur and to realise how unnecessary are Pamphilus' and Myrrina's attempts to prevent knowledge of the pregnancy from spreading, and how ill directed are the young man's desperate efforts to avoid its consequences when it does force its way into the open. On the Apollodoran scheme, therefore, we see a huge injection of humour derived from the misunderstandings and embarrassment of the stage characters. This Terence converted into suspense and anxiety when he denied his audience that element of impartial exposition.

A further repercussion of Terence's technique comes in the reaction of the audience to the characters themselves, and to Pamphilus in particular. In the Greek play he was known to be a rapist virtually from the outset; in Terence the distaste that might have been engendered by such knowledge, and which Menander strove to counter in *Epitrepontes* (see below), is avoided by delaying its actual revelation until the very moment of reconciliation, when the initial wrong can be righted. What we see as a result is not a young man so taken up with his own predicament that his attitude to his wife appears both uncaring and hypocritical, but a sharing of the young wife's misery which comes across as both credible and worthy of some sympathy.

Omission of the original expository prologue by Terence did not, however, remove the need for exposition altogether, and commentators have been much exercised in their attempts to locate within the Roman play those sections where the playwright has supposedly attempted to compensate for his innovation. So for instance, Lefèvre p.60ff., drawing upon the arguments of others, posits a number of places in which he claims to see evidence of original prologue material inserted by Terence into the body of the Roman play: 1) Parmeno's narrative 114-75, 2) Pamphilus' monologue 361ff., in particular 383 & 393-5, 3) Myrrina's monologue 566-76, in particular 572-4, and 4) Bacchis' monologue 816ff. In none of these cases, however, is scholarly opinion united (Kuiper p.7f. n.7, Sewart[1] p.138ff., [3] p.251f.). No less problematic are scenes in which it is claimed Terence altered the format of Apollodorus' play by conversion of dramatic action into narrative. The two principal instances involve the monologue of Pamphilus at 361ff. and that spoken by Bacchis towards the play's end, at 816ff. In the case of the first the description of Myrrina's appeals to her son-in-law has frequently been seen as replacing what in the original was enacted by an encounter onstage (Schadewaldt p.13ff., Denzler p.69ff., Carney *ad loc*.). Against this, however, Jachmann p.640 pointed to the impropriety of having a married woman brought to her knees before her son-in-law, especially if the Greek audience knew him to be a rapist. More seriously Sewart[1] p.39ff. demonstrates that the hypothesis of such an onstage encounter between Pamphilus and Myrrina has far reaching effects not only on this scene but on others as well. If Terence has here converted dialogue into monologue, he must also have altered the previous scene with Parmeno and Sostrata since Pamphilus' reticence there is founded upon a promise he had already given Myrrina. Alternatively, if portrayal of the actual encounter with Myrrina follows the meeting with Sostrata, it is effectively rendered otiose, since Pamphilus' answers to his mother's questions indicate he has already determined upon silence without the intervention of his mother-in-law. Thus Sewart[1] p.45

12

concludes "The alterations necessary to establish a Pamphilus/Myrrina dialogue firmly within the framework of surrounding scenes are so great as to demand completely different roles for both Parmeno and Sostrata in a Greek original which would bear little resemblance to the Hecyra of Terence".

If the basis for restructuring events in 361ff. was subjective interpretation by modern commentators, that at 816ff. goes back to Donatus, who ostensibly had access to Apollodorus' play. In a note on 816 itself, for example, he writes "the remaining part of the plot is related by means of a monody", while later on 825 he states "Terence has had regard for conciseness; for in the Greek play these things are acted out, not narrated", and on 833 we find "he has rounded off the story in his usual way, with narrative, so that we might not wait for this later in the play". Yet while the fact of alteration has been generally accepted, detailed interpretation of its form has displayed wide variation. Some writers for instance suggested for the Greek play a dialogue between Bacchis and Pamphilus on the events that had occurred nine months earlier; others a scene at the beginning of the play in which the dialogue between Bacchis and Pamphilus narrated at 824ff. was actually depicted; others still a scene between Bacchis and Myrrina, who happened to come onstage just at the right moment, or between Bacchis and Parmeno (see Marti[2] p.54f.). Eventually, of the various permutations offered, a dialogue between Bacchis and Myrrina, first proposed by Nencini, came to represent the favoured option.

Once again, however, Sewart[1] p.63ff. has called into question the whole basis of previous argument, claiming that there is in fact no compelling internal reason for a meeting between Bacchis and any other character at this point and that the sequence of scenes found in Terence's play is in essence superior to any alternative offered. As to the external evidence provided by Donatus Sewart[1] p.92ff. argues that in general an incorrect interpretation has been imposed upon the statements of the commentator. The note on 816 for instance becomes a reference not to the change from dialogue to narrative but from the vagueness of 811f. to the clear revelation of the truth in the monologue, and therefore of little relevance to the format of the Greek original. In the case of 833 the cause of difficulties is seen as residing in unnecessary emendation of the manuscript reading: *conclusit narrationem fabulae more suo*: "he has rounded off the explanation of events in his usual way...", which may be no more than a comment on the playwright tying up loose ends. The emended text on the other hand: *conclusit narratione fabulam more suo*: "he has rounded off the story in his usual way, with narrative..." Sewart argues makes little sense, since it was clearly not Terence's practice to end his plays in this way. Finally on 825 Sewart concludes (p.109) from a survey of Donatus' commentary as a whole either that the statement "in the Greek play these things are acted out, not narrated" is a post-Donatus insertion, or that the whole note should be seen as a reference not to Terence but to Apollodorus and interpreted as "the writer of the play (sc. Apollodorus) has consulted the interests of brevity for in a Greek play it is customary that such a scene of recognition be acted out before the audience and not merely reported as here".

For all the astuteness of such arguments, however, acceptance of Donatus' testimony at face value continues to dominate scholarly thinking. Thus Goldberg in his recent book p.159 writes "By compressing the actual recognition into a monologue and thereby reducing the amount of stage time devoted to it, Terence minimizes the importance of its contribution to the plot and willingly forfeits much of its traditional comic value." Such variety of opinion illustrates graphically indeed the difficulty involved in any attempt to analyse in detail those alterations Terence may have introduced into his Greek original. It is not that one commentator is demonstrably right, another wrong, merely that the nature of the evidence involved, its potential for a wide spectrum of subjective interpretation, ensures that diversity of conclusion becomes inevitable.

THE MOTHER-IN-LAW AND THE *EPITREPONTES* OF MENANDER

In the absence of the Apollodoran original of *Hecyra* the affinities that exist between Terence's play and Menander's *Epitrepontes* (*Arbitration*) have often been used to provide insight into the varying concerns and approaches of the two playwrights (Goldberg p.150ff., Sewart[1] p.196ff.). At one time indeed the similarities they display were interpreted as indicating a direct influence upon Terence by the Menandrian drama. It was a hypothesis, we have to admit, born more of the elation that greeted the rediscovery of Greek New Comedy in the early decades of this century than of any certain insight, and as a result is no longer accepted. Nevertheless, a comparison of the two does help reveal shifts of technique and effect that are of value in gauging the degree of success with which Terence presents his own drama.

In both plays the underlying situation which constitutes the plot is founded upon the breakdown of a marriage through the birth of seemingly illegitimate children, in each case the result of rape. Faced with this, the young husbands involved feel themselves unable to continue living with their wives until the discovery that they are themselves the rapists. In *Epitrepontes*, though only about half the play survives and the first Act is almost totally lost, there is little doubt that an expository prologue existed to inform the audience of the fact upon which the main effect of dramatic irony is built - Charisios' responsibility for the pregnancy. Without such knowledge many subsequent events portrayed onstage simply lose both their poignancy and much of their humour.

As to the actual events portrayed the major points of divergence between the two plays centre upon their approach to the question of rape, the attitude of the young hero to what he discovers, and the extent to which the truth of the situation is eventually allowed to become common knowledge among stage characters. As already stated, the revelation at the beginning of *Epitrepontes* that Charisios is a rapist demands from Menander a conscious effort to mitigate its implications in terms of audience sympathy. This the playwright largely achieves through his treatment of the wronged wife, Pamphile, whose rebuttal of her father's attempts to effect what amounts to a divorce, a rebuttal couched in terms of affection and tolerance for her husband's own apparent involvement with another woman, is overheard by the young man himself. The effect upon Charisios, already in turmoil over rejection of his wife and convinced that he too is the father of an illegitimate child by the music-girl Habrotonon, is overwhelming. Filled with remorse at his earlier unfeeling reaction to his wife's supposed infidelity he rails at himself, 895ff.: "Look at me, the villain. I myself commit a crime like this, and am the father of a bastard child. Yet I felt not a scrap of mercy, showed none to that woman in the same sad fortune. I'm a heartless brute." cf. 908ff.: "A faultless man, eyes fixed on his good name, a judge of what is right and what is wrong, in his own life pure and beyond reproach - my image, which some power above has well and quite correctly shattered. Here I showed that I was human. 'Wretched worm, in pose and talk so bumptious, you won't tolerate a woman's forced misfortune. I shall show that you have stumbled just the same yourself. Then *she* will treat you tenderly, while *you* insult her. You'll appear unlucky, rude, a heartless brute, too, all at once.' Did she address her father then as you'd have done? 'I'm here' she said, 'to share his life. Mishaps occur. I mustn't run away'." (trans. Arnott). Such self-analysis and criticism does much in fact to rescue Charisios from the charge of hypocrisy and insensitivity. In the case of *The Mother-in-Law*'s Pamphilus on the other hand that growing self-awareness never materialises, replaced instead by the young man's attempts to spare Philumena the effects of her disgrace becoming common knowledge, but as a result the happy ending is robbed of what might have added greatly to its poignancy.

By the end of Act IV of *Epitrepontes* comes the realisation that through the intervention of comic coincidence the supposedly illegitimate offspring of Charisios and Pamphile are one and the same baby. In Act V this information is conveyed to the girl's father, Smikrines, both in order to discomfit the old man for his earlier interference, and no doubt, though the text in fact gives out at this point, to include him in the general celebration that formed the conclusion of many New Comedy plays. In *The Mother-in-Law* on the other hand, as Goldberg observes p.166, though the action of the play has laid stress upon the difficulties that beset the older generation, and Myrrina and Sostrata in particular, the play ends with the resolution of only their children's problems. Certainly neither woman is given any overt recompense for the tribulations she has suffered (cf. Chrysis in Menander's *Samia*), and the discomfiture of Laches and Phidippus demanded by natural justice for their earlier ill-tempered outbursts fails to materialise; instead it is pointedly rejected as a possibility in the interests of what is evidently intended to be a more naturalistic outcome.

METRE

The Metres of Terence

The whole of Roman Comedy, like its Greek predecessor, is written in verse form, the varying metres used indicating different degrees of liveliness with which the lines were delivered and the presence or absence of musical accompaniment. *The Mother-in-Law* itself contains none of the songs from the actors such as are found in Plautine comedy or occur as isolated instances in Terence's *Andria* 481-4, 626-38, and *Adelphoe* 610-7 (see further Duckworth[2] p.362ff.). It consists instead of spoken verse in iambic senarii, which occupy some 40% of the play, or more rhythmical lines declaimed as a form of 'recitative' to the accompaniment of the pipe. The basis for all such metrical forms is the syllable, scanned not by stress but by length. In their simplest forms they may be represented as follows:

Iambic senarius	v- v- v- v- v- v-
Iambic septenarius	v- v- v- v- v- v- v- v
Iambic octonarius	v- v- v- v- v- v- v- v-
Iambic dimeter catalectic	v- v- v- v
Trochaic septenarius	-v -v -v -v -v -v -v -
Trochaic octonarius	-v -v -v -v -v -v -v -v
Trochaic dimeter catalectic	-v -v -v -

More often than not, however, we find variation caused by:
1. The possibility of transforming most iambi and trochees into spondees, - -.
2. Resolution of long syllables into two shorts to produce tribrachs: vvv, dactyls: -vv, anapaests: vv-, or proceleusmatics: vvvv.
Further variation occurs as a result of numerous additional factors, among which are:
1. Elision: a final vowel or a final syllable ending in 'm' is discounted if the following word begins with a vowel or a syllable beginning with 'h'. Related to this is prodelision whereby *est* and *es* may lose their vowel by coalescing with the word that precedes them, e.g. *datast* 1, *planest* 5, *licitumst* 30, *exanimatu's* 825.

2. Synizesis: two contiguous vowels not normally coalescing to form a diphthong may in fact do so.

3. The possibility of discounting a final 's' if this would result in the lengthening of an otherwise short syllable. In disyllabic words ending in 'e' the loss of this letter is also occasionally found.

4. The law of *brevis brevians* or iambic shortening whereby a long syllable is shortened if it is both directly preceded by a short syllable and directly preceded and/or followed by a syllable with word-accent.

(On comic metres in general see Willcock p.141ff., Raven p.47ff., Duckworth[2] p.364ff. For those of Terence see Ashmore p.49ff., Gratwick p.268ff.)

The Metrical Pattern of *The Mother-in-Law*

The following represents the major metrical forms used in scenes:

Act	Lines	Scene	Metre
I	1-57	Prologues	iamb sen
	58-197	Philotis Syra Parmeno	iamb sen
II	198-242	Laches Sostrata	iamb oct/sen - troch sept
	243-273	Phidippus Laches Sostrata	iamb sept
	274-80	Sostrata	troch sept
III	281-335	Pamphilus Parmeno	troch oct/sept - iamb oct/sept - iamb sen
	336-60	Sostrata Parmeno Pamphilus	iamb sept
	361-414	Pamphilus	troch sept - iamb sen
	415-50	Parmeno Sosia Pamphilus	iamb sen

	451-515	Laches Phidippus Pamphilus	troch sept - iamb sen
IV	516-76	Myrrina Phidippus	troch oct/sept - iamb oct
	576-606	Sostrata Pamphilus	iamb oct
	607-22	Laches Sostrata Pamphilus	iamb sept/sen troch sept/oct
	623-726	Phidippus Laches Pamphilus	iamb sen
V	727-67	Bacchis Laches	iamb oct/sept troch sept/oct
	768-98	Phidippus Laches Bacchis	iamb sept
	799-840	Parmeno Bacchis	troch sept iamb sept
	841-80	Pamphilus Parmeno Bacchis	troch oct/sept

The basic metrical pattern of the play is one of alternating iambic and trochaic rhythms either between scenes or within scenes. Of these the most prosaic, the iambic senarius, occurs at reasonably appreciable length on six occasions: 1) the Prologues 1-57, 2) the expository scenes of Philotis Syra and Parmeno 58-197, 3) Parmeno's reasons for not following Pamphilus into Phidippus' house 327-35, 4) Pamphilus' reintroduction of Parmeno and interaction with him 409-50, 5) Pamphilus' defence of Philumena and Phidippus' resulting anger 485-515, 6) the forcing of Pamphilus into his final corner 623-726. Of these the clarity and simplicity of the senarius is clearly the controlling factor in 1, 2, 3, 6 and perhaps 4, though here and in 5 the contrast to be achieved by variation with trochaic rhythms must also be an important element.

Elsewhere the introduction of longer lines in iambic or trochaic rhythms with their musical accompaniment injects an element of both variety (Acts II & V) and raised emotional tone: the highly charged events of Act II and the opening of Act III, for instance, or the equally emotive events with which Act IV opens. That Terence also deliberately replaced the iambic trimeters of some scenes in the Greek original with trochaic septenarii is not only suggested by the increased frequency of this metre in the Roman plays in general, but is confirmed by those places like 286f. where the text of Apollodorus has been preserved.

If the introduction of the trochaic septenarius is often to be explained by its popularity and usefulness as an alternative for the senarius, its counterpart in iambic metre seems designed in this play at least for the production of suspense, as suggested by the scenes where it occurs: 1) Phidippus' failure to account for Philumena's refusal to return to her rightful home, which frustrates Laches' hopes for an early resolution of the situation 243-73, 2) Sostrata's intervention at 336-60, which increases the tension of Pamphilus' presence in Phidippus' house and then delays the young man's revelation of the truth, 3) the initial shadow-boxing between Laches and Bacchis 732-42, 4) the return of Phidippus bringing the nurse, which delays Bacchis' approach to Myrrina 769-97.

THE TEXT

The text adopted here is essentially that of Lindsay and Kauer, though without the marks added to their Oxford edition to facilitate scansion. Similarly the practice of dropping final 's' after a short vowel and before an initial consonant has here been restricted to the penultimate syllables of lines, where to do otherwise might mislead. This wish to avoid confusion also accounts for those instances where final 'e' has been dropped or where *-us es* has been printed as *-u's*.

Differences of text (excluding punctuation and spelling) between this edition and Lindsay-Kauer occur at: *Didascalia* I 6, *Didascalia* II 1, *Hecyra* 64, 134, 160, 208, 220, 258, 288, 629, 643, 661, 666-7, 791, 880.

ABBREVIATIONS USED IN THE APPARATUS CRITICUS

A : Codex Bembinus, written in rustic capitals, 4th/5th c. Though lacking lines 1-37 of *Hecyra*, A stands out as by far the oldest manuscript of Terence, and thus less affected by the emendations and interpolations that have crept into the rest of the MSS tradition. However, the presence in A of errors not found elsewhere prevents its testimony being accepted uncritically in every instance.

Σ : The agreement of manuscripts (over 600) other than A. They are all of either mediaeval or Renaissance date, but derive ultimately from a recension by a figure who styled himself Calliopius, though exactly when and where this was produced is unknown. Errors common to A and Σ argue powerfully for their common origin in a single lost archetype, usually designated Φ (see further Grant p.3ff.).

Jov.: Joviales, a 6th c. corrector of A introducing changes derived from the Calliopian branch of the manuscript tradition.

γ: The agreement of CPFE, minuscule manuscripts of the 9th-11th c. (C: Codex Vaticanus 9th c., P: Parisinus 7899 9th c., F: Ambrosianus 10th c., E: Riccardianus 11th c.).

δ: the agreement of DGLp, minuscule manuscripts of the 10th-11th c. (D: Codex Victorianus 10th c., G: Decurtatus 11th c., L: Lipsiensis 10th c., p: Parisinus 10304 10th c.).

C^1 etc.: the first hand in C. C^2 etc.: corrections to C by another hand.

Don. Donatus, 4th c. commentator on the plays of Terence. Much of his work displays signs of later addition by other writers and at times produces more problems for understanding than it does solutions.

Modern editions referred to in either the Apparatus Criticus or Commentary include:

Bentley (Cambridge 1726, Amsterdam 1727)
Fleckeisen (Leipzig 1857, 1898, 1916-7)
Umpfenbach (Berlin 1870)
Dziatzko (Leipzig 1884)
Ashmore (New York 1908^2)
Sargeaunt (London & Harvard 1912)
Marouzeau (Paris 1947-9)
Stella (Milan 1972 = 1952^2)
Carney (Salisbury, Rhodesia 1963)

TERENCE

The Mother-in-Law

HECYRA

DIDASCALIA

I (secundum A)

INCIPIT TERENTI HECYRA. ACTA LUDIS MEGALENSIBUS
SEXTO IULIO CAESARE CN. CORNELIO DOLABELLA
AEDILIBUS CURULIBUS.
MODOS FECIT FLACCUS CLAUDI TIBIS PARIBUS TOTA.
5   GRAECA MENANDRU. FACTA EST V.
ACTA PRIMO SINE PROLOGO CN. OCTAVIO TITO MANLIO COS.
RELATA EST LUCIO AEMILIO PAULO LUDIS FUNERALIBUS;
NON EST PLACITA.
TERTIO RELATA EST Q. FULVIO
10   LUC. MARCIO AEDILIBUS CURULIBUS.
EGIT LUC. AMBIVIUS LUC. SERGIUS TURPIO; PLACUIT.

II (secundum codices praeter A)

INCIPIT HECYRA. ACTA LUDIS MEGALENSIBUS
SEX. IUL. CAES. CN. CORNELIO AEDILIBUS CURULIBUS.
NON EST PERACTA.
MODOS FECIT FLACCUS CLAUDI TIBIIS PARILIBUS TOTA;
5   CN. OCTAVIO T. MANLIO COS.
RELATA EST ITERUM L. AEMILIO PAULO LUDIS FUNERALIBUS.
RELATA EST TERTIO Q. FULVIO L. MARTIO AEDIL. CURUL.

The Mother-in-Law

Production Notice

1 (According to MS A)

Here begins *The Mother-in-Law* by Terence. Performed at the Megalensian Games when Sextus Julius Caesar and Gnaeus Cornelius Dolabella were Curule Aediles. Music throughout for the double pipe by Flaccus, (slave) of Claudius. (5) Greek by Menander. Terence's fifth play. First staged without prologue in the consulships of Gnaeus Octavius and Titus Manlius. Repeated at the Funeral Games in honour of Lucius Aemilius Paulus. It was not a success. Repeated for the third time when Quintus Fulvius and (10) Lucius Marcius were Curule Aediles. Produced by Lucius Ambivius (and) Lucius Sergius Turpio. It proved successful.

2 (According to MSS other than A)

Here begins *The Mother-in-Law*. Performed at the Megalensian Games when Sextus Julius Caesar and Gnaeus Cornelius were Curule Aediles. It was not acted through to the end. Music throughout for the double pipe by Flaccus (slave) of Claudius. (5) The consuls were Gnaeus Octavius and Titus Manlius. Repeated at the Funeral Games for Lucius Aemilius Paulus. Repeated for the third time when Quintus Fulvius and Lucius Martius were Curule Aediles.

24

C. SULPICI APOLLINARIS PERIOCHA

Uxorem ducit Pamphilus Philumenam,
cui quondam ignorans virgini vitium obtulit,
cuiusque per vim quem detraxit anulum
dederat amicae Bacchidi meretriculae.
5   dein profectus in Imbrum est; nuptam haud attigit.
hanc mater utero gravidam, ne id sciat socrus,
ut aegram ad sese transfert. revenit Pamphilus,
deprendit partum, celat; uxorem tamen
recipere non volt. pater incusat Bacchidis
10   amorem. dum se purgat Bacchis, anulum
mater vitiatae forte adgnoscit Myrrina.
uxorem recipit Pamphilus cum filio.

PERSONAE

(Prologus)	Sostrata Matrona
Philotis Meretrix	Phidippus Senex
Syra Anus	Pamphilus Adulescens
Parmeno Servos	Sosia Servos
(Scirtus Servos)	Myrrina Matrona
Laches Senex	Bacchis Meretrix

The Summary of Gaius Sulpicius Apollinaris

Pamphilus marries Philumena whom earlier, while she was still a virgin, he raped
without knowing who she was. A ring of hers, which he had seized from her by
force, he gave to his girlfriend, the courtesan Bacchis. (5) Subsequently he set out
for Imbros without having consummated his marriage. The girl, now pregnant,
was taken back to her own home by her mother on the pretext of being ill so that
her mother-in-law might not learn of her condition. Pamphilus returns, discovers
the birth and keeps it secret, but refuses to take his wife back. His father blames
the affair with Bacchis. (10) While Bacchis is defending herself against the
charge, the raped girl's mother, Myrrina, happens to recognise the ring. Pamphilus
takes back his wife and his son.

CHARACTERS

(Prologue speaker)   Sostrata, wife
Philotis, courtesan   Phidippus, old man
Syra, old woman   Pamphilus, young man
Parmeno, slave   Sosia, slave
(Scirtus, slave)   Myrrina, wife
Laches, old man   Bacchis, courtesan

PROLOGUS (I)

Hecyra est huic nomen fabulae. haec quom datast
nova, novom intervenit vitium et calamitas
ut neque spectari neque cognosci potuerit:
ita populus studio stupidus in funambulo
5   animum occuparat. nunc haec planest pro nova,
et is qui scripsit hanc ob eam rem noluit
iterum referre ut iterum possit vendere.
alias cognostis eius: quaeso hanc noscite.

PROLOGUS (II)

Orator ad vos venio ornatu prologi.
10   sinite exorator sim eodem ut iure uti senem
liceat quo iure sum usus adulescentior,
novas qui exactas feci ut inveterascerent,
ne cum poeta scriptura evanesceret.
in is quas primum Caecili didici novas
15   partim sum earum exactus, partim vix steti.
quia scibam dubiam fortunam esse scaenicam,
spe incerta certum mihi laborem sustuli;
easdem agere coepi ut ab eodem alias discerem
novas, studiose ne illum ab studio abducerem.
20   perfeci ut spectarentur. ubi sunt cognitae,
placitae sunt. ita poetam restitui in locum
prope iam remotum iniuria advorsarium
ab studio atque ab labore atque arte musica.
quod si scripturam sprevissem in praesentia
25   et in deterrendo voluissem operam sumere,
ut in otio esset potius quam in negotio,
deterruissem facile ne alias scriberet.
nunc quid petam mea causa aequo animo attendite:

Prologue I

The title of this play is *The Mother-in-Law*. When first staged it was interrupted by a singularly inauspicious event and misfortune, with the result that it could be neither viewed nor given a fair hearing. The audience in fact, all agog with eagerness, had its attention fixed upon a tight-rope walker. (5) Its presentation today, therefore, is clearly by way of a new play, and its author didn't wish to restage it just so he could offer it for sale a second time. You are acquainted with his other plays; now, I beg you, view the present one.

Prologue II

I come before you dressed as prologue-speaker to plead a case. (10) Allow me to succeed with my plea so that in my old age I can enjoy the same privilege as in my younger days, when I caused new plays that had been driven from the stage to become established favourites, and thus prevented such works from fading into oblivion along with their author. Take for instance the early productions of Caecilius I first acted in; (15) with some of them I was driven from the stage, with others I hardly held my ground. Because, however, I knew the theatre was a risky business, I undertook the certainty of hard work with no certainty of success. I began to stage those same plays in order to secure other, fresh scripts from the same author, and stage them to my best endeavour so as not to discourage him from his endeavours. (20) I managed to get them performed, and once they had been given a hearing they proved successful. In this way I restored to his rightful place a playwright whom the ill-will of his opponents had well-nigh driven from his calling, his occupation and from dramatic art. But if at the time I had rejected his works (25) and had chosen instead to spare no effort in discouraging him so that he spent his time in idleness rather than employment, I could easily have discouraged him from writing other plays. But now, for my sake, grant a fair hearing to my request.

28

Hecyram ad vos refero, quam mihi per silentium
30 numquam agere licitumst; ita eam oppressit calamitas.
eam calamitatem vostra intellegentia
sedabit si erit adiutrix nostrae industriae.
quom primum eam agere coepi, pugilum gloria -
funambuli eodem accessit exspectatio -
35 comitum conventus, strepitus, clamor mulierum
fecere ut ante tempus exirem foras.
vetere in nova coepi uti consuetudine
in experiundo ut essem; refero denuo.
primo actu placeo. quom interea rumor venit
40 datum iri gladiatores, populus convolat,
tumultuantur, clamant, pugnant de loco;
ego interea meum non potui tutari locum.
nunc turba nulla est; otium et silentiumst;
agendi tempus mihi datumst, vobis datur
45 potestas condecorandi ludos scaenicos.
nolite sinere per vos artem musicam
recidere ad paucos; facite ut vostra auctoritas
meae auctoritati fautrix adiutrixque sit.
si numquam avare pretium statui arti meae
50 et eum esse quaestum in animum induxi maxumum
quam maxume servire vostris commodis,
sinite impetrare me, qui in tutelam meam
studium suom et se in vostram commisit fidem,
ne eum circumventum inique iniqui inrideant.
55 mea causa causam accipite et date silentium,
ut lubeat scribere aliis mihique ut discere
novas expediat posthac pretio emptas meo.

Once more I bring before you *The Mother-in-Law*, a play **(30)** I have never been allowed to present in silence: so dogged by misfortune has it been. That misfortune, however, your good sense will eliminate if it lends its support to our efforts. When I began presenting it on the first occasion, talk of a boxing-match - there was also the prospect of a tight-rope walker at the same venue - **(35)** crowds of supporters, uproar, and the screaming of women all forced me to leave the stage before the end. With this new play I undertook to follow my old practice and try again. I staged it a second time. In the first part I met with success, but then came a rumour **(40)** there was to be a gladiatorial display: in flocked the people, pushing and shoving, shouting, jostling for places. In all of this I couldn't maintain my own place.

Today, however, there is no tumult; all is peace and quiet. For my part I have the chance to present the play, you **(45)** the opportunity to bestow honour upon the dramatic festivals. Don't allow yourselves to be responsible for dramatic art falling into the hands of only a few; ensure that your judgement both aids and abets my own. If I have never set an excessive price upon my profession, **(50)** and have always regarded serving your interests to the best of my ability as my highest reward, grant me that the playwright, who has entrusted his work to my safe-keeping and himself to your sense of fair-dealing, may not be cheated and unjustly derided by unjust individuals. **(55)** For my sake heed this plea of mine and listen in silence so that others may be encouraged to write, and I find it profitable in future to present new plays purchased at my own expense.

(I i) **Philotis Syra**

PH. Per pol quam paucos reperias meretricibus
  fidelis evenire amatores, Syra!
60 vel hic Pamphilus iurabat quotiens Bacchidi,
  quam sancte, ut quivis facile posset credere,
  numquam illa viva ducturum uxorem domum.
  em, duxit. **SY**. ergo propterea te sedulo
  et moneo et hortor ne quoiusquam misereas,
65 quin spolies mutiles laceres quemque nacta sis.
  PH. utine eximium neminem habeam? **SY**. neminem;
  nam nemo illorum quisquam, scito, ad te venit
  quin ita paret sese abs te ut blanditiis suis
  quam minimo pretio suam voluptatem expleat.
70 hiscin tu amabo non contra insidiabere?
  PH. tamen pol eandem iniuriumst esse omnibus.
  SY. iniurium autem est ulcisci advorsarios,
  aut qua via te captent eadem ipsos capi?
  eheu me miseram! quor non aut istaec mihi
75 aetas et formast aut tibi haec sententia?

(I ii) **Parmeno Philotis Syra**

PAR. Senex si quaeret me, modo isse dicito
  ad portum percontatum adventum Pamphili.
  audin quid dicam, Scirte? si quaeret me, uti
  tum dicas; si non quaeret, nullus dixeris,
80 alias ut uti possim causa hac integra.
  sed videon ego Philotium? unde haec ، venit?
  Philotis, salve multum. **PH**. o salve, Parmeno.
  SY. salve mecastor, Parmeno. **PAR**. et tu edepol, Syra.
  dic mi, ubi, Philotis, te oblectasti tam diu?

A street-scene in Athens; by convention, the side entrance to the left leads to the harbour, that on the right to the forum, the market place. Before us stand three house-doors: one belonging to Laches, another to Phidippus, the third to Bacchis, through which emerge two women in conversation.

PHILOTIS: Goodness me, how very few lovers you find turn out faithful to their mistresses, Syra! **(60)** Take Pamphilus here for instance. *(Indicates the house belonging to Laches)* No end of times he swore to Bacchis that as long as she was alive he'd never take a wife, and with such solemnity anyone might easily have believed him. Well, he's got married.

SYRA: And that's exactly why I'm forever telling you and urging you not to take pity on any of them. **(65)** Instead, once you get your hands on one of them, take him to the cleaners, fleece him, rob him blind.

PHILOTIS: Do you mean I'm to make no exceptions?

SYRA: Not a one. None of them, after all, comes to you without being prepared to charm you into satisfying his desires at the least possible price. Of that you may be sure. **(70)** Well then, aren't you going to set your own traps for them in turn?

PHILOTIS: And yet, surely it's wrong to treat them all the same.

SYRA: What? Is it wrong to get your own back on your enemies, or for them to be cheated in the same way they try to catch you out? Dear me! If only I had **(75)** your years and looks, or else you had my sense.

(Parmeno emerges from Laches' house addressing a fellow slave still inside)

(I ii)

PARMENO: If the old man asks for me, say I've just gone to the harbour to make enquiries about Pamphilus' return. Do you hear what I'm saying, Scirtus? If he asks for me, tell him then. If he doesn't ask, don't say a word, **(80)** so I can keep the excuse for use some other time. *(Turns and notices the women)* But is that Philotis I see? Where's she appeared from? Philotis, how nice to see you!

PHILOTIS: Why Parmeno, how are you?

SYRA: Good morning, Parmeno.

PARMENO: And good morning to you too, Syra. Tell me, Philotis, where have you been amusing yourself all this time?

85   **PH**. mimime equidem me oblectavi, quae cum milite
        Corinthum hinc sum profecta inhumanissimo.
        biennium ibi perpetuom misera illum tuli.
        PAR. edepol te desiderium Athenarum arbitror,
        Philotium, cepisse saepe et te tuom
90   consilium contempsisse. **PH**. non dici potest
        quam cupida eram huc redeundi, abeundi a milite
        vosque hic videndi, antiqua ut consuetudine
        agitarem inter vos libere convivium.
        nam illi haud licebat nisi praefinito loqui
95   quae illi placerent. **PAR**. haud opinor commode
        finem statuisse orationi militem.
        PH. sed quid hoc negotist? modo quae narravit mihi
        hic intus Bacchis? quod ego numquam credidi
        fore, ut ille hac viva posset animum inducere
100   uxorem habere. **PAR**. habere autem? **PH**. eho tu, an non habet?
        PAR. habet, sed firmae hae vereor ut sint nuptiae.
        PH. ita di deaeque faxint, si in rem est Bacchidis!
        sed qui istuc credam ita esse dic mihi, Parmeno.
        PAR. non est opus prolato hoc; percontarier
105   desiste. **PH**. nempe ea causa, ut ne id fiat palam?
        ita me di amabunt, haud propterea te rogo,
        ut hoc proferam, sed ut tacita mecum gaudeam.
        PAR. numquam tam dices commode ut tergum meum
        tuam in fidem committam. **PH**. ah noli, Parmeno!
110   quasi tu non multo malis narrare hoc mihi
        quam ego quae percontor scire. **PAR**. vera haec praedicat
        et illud mihi vitiumst maxumum. si mihi fidem
        das te tacituram, dicam. **PH**. ad ingenium redis.
        fidem do; loquere. **PAR**. ausculta. **PH**. istic sum.

PHILOTIS: (85) I've been anything but amusing myself. I went off to Corinth with a complete boor of a soldier, and for two whole years I've had the misfortune of putting up with him there.

PARMENO: Yes, and I'm sure you often longed for Athens and (90) regretted that decision of yours, Philotis dear.

PHILOTIS: I can't tell you how much I yearned to come back, escape that soldier and see you all here, so I could go the rounds of entertainment among you, free and easy, just like in the old days. There I couldn't say a word except, as was made abundantly clear, (95) the kind of thing that pleased him.

PARMENO: No, I don't suppose the soldier's setting a limit to your chatter was much to your taste.

PHILOTIS: But what's going on? What's this that Bacchis has just been telling me inside? I never would have believed it possible that Pamphilus would take it into his head to get married while she was still alive. (100)

PARMENO: Married, do you say?

PHILOTIS: Come now, isn't he married?

PARMENO: He is, but I'm afraid it isn't a very stable marriage.

PHILOTIS: I hope to God it isn't, if that's to Bacchis' advantage! But give me one good reason for thinking that's how it is, Parmeno.

PARMENO: It's not something to be spread around, so don't ask. (105)

PHILOTIS: You mean so that it doesn't become common knowledge? Heaven preserve me, that's not why I'm asking - to spread it around - but for my own private pleasure. I won't breathe a word.

PARMENO: *(Backs off)* You can be as persuasive as you like, but I'll not trust *my* back to *your* word of honour.

PHILOTIS: Don't give me that, Parmeno! (110) As if you weren't far more eager to tell me the facts than I am to get answers to my questions.

PARMENO: *(Aside)* It's true what she says - that's my greatest failing. *(Aloud)* Well, I'll tell if you promise not to breathe a word.

PHILOTIS: There, you're becoming your old self again. I promise. Go on.

PARMENO: Listen.

PHILOTIS: I'm with you.

PAR. hanc Bacchidem
115   amabat ut quom maxume tum Pamphilus
quom pater uxorem ut ducat orare occipit
et haec communia omnium quae sunt patrum,
sese senem esse dicere, illum autem unicum;
praesidium velle se senectuti suae.
120   ill' primo se negare; sed postquam acrius
pater instat, fecit animi ut incertus foret
pudorin anne amori obsequeretur magis.
tundendo atque odio denique effecit senex;
despondit ei gnatam huius vicini proxumi.
125   usque illud visum est Pamphilo ne utiquam grave
donec iam in ipsis nuptiis, postquam videt
paratas nec moram ullam quin ducat dari.
ibi demum ita aegre tulit ut ipsam Bacchidem,
si adesset, credo ibi eius commiseresceret.
130   ubiquomque datum erat spatium solitudinis
ut conloqui mecum una posset: "Parmeno,
perii, quid ego egi! in quod me conieci malum!
non potero ferre hoc, Parmeno; perii miser."
PH. at te di deaeque perduint cum isto odio, Lache!
135   PAR. ut ad pauca redeam, uxorem deducit domum.
nocte illa prima virginem non attigit;
quae consecutast nox eam, nihilo magis.
PH. quid ais? cum virgine una adulescens cubuerit
plus potus, sese illa abstinere ut potuerit?
140   non veri simile dicis neque verum arbitror.
PAR. credo ita videri tibi; nam nemo ad te venit
nisi cupiens tui. ille invitus illam duxerat.
PH. quid deinde fit? PAR. diebus sane pauculis
post Pamphilus me solum seducit foras

PARMENO: (115) Pamphilus was just as head-over-heels in love with Bacchis here as ever, but then his father started pleading with him to take a wife, using the same old arguments all fathers do: that he was getting on in years, and Pamphilus was his only son, that he wanted some security for his old age. (120) At first Pamphilus refused outright, but when his father pressed him more forcibly, it made him uncertain whether he should follow his duty or his love. By keeping on at him and pestering him the old man finally got his way and betrothed him to the daughter of his next-door neighbour here. *(Indicates Phidippus' house)* (125) For his part Pamphilus didn't take the matter at all seriously - right up until the day of the actual wedding when he saw the preparations were made and there was nothing for it but to get married. Then at last it struck home with such force even Bacchis herself, I think, would have pitied him then, if she'd been there. (130) Whenever he had the chance to be on his own so he could talk to me, he'd say: "Parmeno, I'm ruined! What have I done? What a mess I've got myself into! I won't be able to stand it, Parmeno. I'm completely and utterly ruined."

PHILOTIS: The gods and goddesses damn you, Laches, you and your pestering! (135)

PARMENO: To cut a long story short, he got married, but that first night he didn't touch the girl; no more he did the following night.

PHILOTIS: *(Astonished)* What's that you're saying? A young man could go to bed with a girl after more than a few drinks and keep his hands off her? (140) That's a likely story; I don't believe it!

PARMENO: I can well understand your reaction. After all, no one comes to you unless he wants you; but *he* married *her* against his will.

PHILOTIS: Well, what happened next?

PARMENO: Just a few days later Pamphilus took me outside in private and told

145   narratque ut virgo ab se integra etiam tum siet,
       seque ante quam eam uxorem duxisset domum,
       sperasse eas tolerare posse nuptias.
       "sed quam decrerim me non posse diutius
       habere, eam ludibrio haberi, Parmeno,
150   quin integram itidem reddam, ut accepi ab suis,
       neque honestum mihi neque utile ipsi virginist."
       PH. pium ac pudicum ingenium narras Pamphili.
       PAR. "hoc ego proferre incommodum mi esse arbitror;
       reddi patri autem, quoi tu nil dicas viti,
155   superbumst. sed illam spero, ubi hoc cognoverit
       non posse se mecum esse, abituram denique."
       PH. quid interea? ibatne ad Bacchidem? PAR. cotidie;
       sed ut fit, postquam hunc alienum ab sese videt,
       maligna multo et mage procax facta ilico est.
160   PH. non edepol mirum. PAR. atqui ea res multo maxume
       diiunxit illum ab illa, postquam et ipse se
       et illam et hanc quae domi erat cognovit satis,
       ad exemplum ambarum mores earum existimans.
       haec, ita uti liberali esse ingenio decet,
165   pudens, modesta, incommoda atque iniurias
       viri omnis ferre et tegere contumelias.
       hic, animus partim uxoris misericordia
       devinctus, partim victus huius iniuriis,
       paullatim elapsust Bacchidi atque huc transtulit
170   amorem, postquam par ingenium nactus est.
       interea in Imbro moritur cognatus senex
       horunc; ea ad hos redibat lege hereditas.
       eo amantem invitum Pamphilum extrudit pater.
       reliquit cum matre hic uxorem; nam senex
175   rus abdidit se, huc raro in urbem commeat.
       PH. quid adhuc habent infirmitatis nuptiae?

me (145) how the girl was still a virgin and that before the wedding he'd hoped he could reconcile himself to the marriage. "But now that I've decided I can't keep her any longer", he said, " it wouldn't be the decent thing on my part, or for the girl's own good, to make her an object of ridicule, Parmeno, (150) rather than return her intact just as I received her from her parents".

PHILOTIS: From your description Pamphilus has a decent side to his character.

PARMENO: Then he said, "I don't think making the situation public would show me in a very good light either, and to return her to her father when there's no fault you could allege against her (155) would smack of insolence. What I'm hoping is that when she realises the impossibility of living with me, she'll eventually just go away".

PHILOTIS: What about things in the meantime? Did he keep on visiting Bacchis?

PARMENO: Every day, but, of course, when she saw he was no longer exclusively hers, she immediately became much harder to get and more exacting in her demands. (160)

PHILOTIS: That comes as no surprise.

PARMENO: But what really broke things up between them was when Pamphilus took stock of himself, of Bacchis, and of the wife he had at home, weighing up the women's characters by the example they both set. His wife was modest and unassuming, as befits a respectable character; (165) she put up with all her husband's unpleasantness and unkind behaviour, kept his insults to herself. Then, with his heart partly won over by feelings of pity for his wife and partly worn down by Bacchis' unkind treatment of him, he gradually drifted away from her and transferred his affections to his wife, (170) since he'd found in her a character like his own. Meanwhile, an elderly relative of theirs died on Imbros, and by law his estate passed to them. Pamphilus was packed off there by his father, much against his will since he was now in love. His wife was left here with his mother: the old man (175) has buried himself away in the country and rarely comes to town.

PHILOTIS: So how in all of this is their marriage on the rocks?

PAR. nunc audies. primo dies complusculos
bene convenibat sane inter eas. interim
miris modis odisse coepit Sostratam:
180 neque lites ullae inter eas, postulatio
numquam. **PH.** quid igitur? **PAR.** siquando ad eam accesserat
confabulatum, fugere e conspectu ilico,
videre nolle. denique ubi non quit pati,
simulat se ad matrem accersi ad rem divinam; abit.
185 ubi illic dies est compluris, accersi iubet:
dixere causam tum nescioquam. iterum iubet:
nemo remisit. postquam accersunt saepius,
aegram esse simulant mulierem. nostra ilico
it visere ad eam: admisit nemo. hoc ubi senex
190 rescivit, heri ea causa rure huc advenit;
patrem continuo convenit Philumenae.
quid egerint inter se nondum etiam scio,
nisi sane curaest quorsum eventurum hoc siet.
habes omnem rem; pergam quo coepi hoc iter.
195 **PH.** et quidem ego; nam constitui cum quodam hospite
me esse illum conventuram. **PAR.** di vortant bene
quod agas! **PH.** vale. **PAR.** et tu bene vale, Philotium.

(II i) Laches Sostrata

LA. Pro deum atque hominum fidem, quod hoc genus est, quae haec est
coniuratio!
utin omnes mulieres eadem aeque studeant nolintque omnia
200 neque declinatam quicquam ab aliarum ingenio ullam reperias!
itaque adeo uno animo omnes socrus oderunt nurus.
viris esse advorsas aeque studiumst, similis pertinaciast,
in eodemque omnes mihi videntur ludo doctae ad malitiam; et
ei ludo, si ullus est, magistram hanc esse satis certo scio.

PARMENO: I'm coming to that. For the first few days all was clearly going well between them, but then the girl developed a strange dislike for Sostrata. **(180)** Not that there was ever any open quarrelling between them or cause for complaint.

PHILOTIS: So what was it?

PARMENO: If ever Sostrata came to have a chat with her, she'd immediately disappear and refuse to see her. Finally, when she couldn't stand the situation any longer, the girl pretended her mother had sent for her to take part in a religious ceremony and off she went. **(185)** After she'd been there several days, Sostrata had her sent for: they pleaded some excuse or other. She sent for her again: no response. After numerous repeated attempts they claimed the girl was ill. Thereupon Mistress went to visit her: no one would let her in. When the old man **(190)** got to hear of it, it brought him up from the country - that was yesterday. Straight away he had a meeting with Philumena's father. What passed between them I don't know as yet, though naturally I'm concerned as to how it'll turn out. So there you have the whole story, and I'll be on my way. **(195)**

PHILOTIS: Me too. I've fixed up an appointment with someone from abroad.

PARMENO: Best of luck with it then.

PHILOTIS: 'Bye. *(Leaves towards town)*

PARMENO: You too, Philotis dear, 'bye.

(Parmeno goes off to the left, the harbour exit. From one of the other two doors Laches bursts onto the stage in a state of considerable agitation, followed with greater hesitation by his wife)

(II i)

LACHES: In the name of gods and men, what a tribe this is, what a conspiracy! Women! They're all the same in their likes and dislikes! **(200)** You can't find a single one of them the least bit different from all the rest in their way of thinking. That's why mothers-in-law are so unanimous in hating their daughters-in-law. They're just as keen, just as persistent when it comes to opposing their husbands. In fact it seems to me they've all had lessons in mischief at the same school, and if there is such a school, I'm quite certain this wife of mine is the headmistress there.

205   SO. me miseram, quae nunc quam ob rem accuser nescio. LA. hem,
     tu nescis? SO. non, ita me di bene ament, mi Lache,
     itaque una inter nos agere aetatem liceat. LA. di mala prohibeant!
     SO. meque abs te inmerito esse accusatam post modo rescisces, scio.
     LA. te inmerito? an quicquam pro istis factis dignum te dici potest,
210   quae me et te et familiam dedecoras, filio luctum paras,
     tum autem ex amicis inimici ut sint nobis adfines facis,
     qui illum decrerunt dignum suos quoi liberos committerent?
     tu sola exorere quae perturbes haec tua inpudentia!
     SO. egon? LA. tu inquam, mulier, quae me omnino lapidem, non
         hominem putas.
215   an, quia ruri esse crebro soleo, nescire arbitramini
     quo quisque pacto hic vitam vostrarum exigat?
     multo melius hic quae fiunt quam illi ubi sum adsidue scio,
     ideo quia, ut vos mihi domi eritis, proinde ego ero fama foris.
     iampridem equidem audivi cepisse odium tui Philumenam,
220   minimeque adeo est mirum, et ni id fecisset mage mirum foret;
     sed non credidi adeo ut etiam totam hanc odisset domum;
     quod si scissem, illa hic maneret potius, tu hinc isses foras.
     at vide quam inmerito aegritudo haec oritur mi abs te, Sostrata:
     rus habitatum abii, concedens vobis et rei serviens,
225   sumptus vostros otiumque ut nostra res posset pati,
     meo labori haud parcens praeter aequom atque aetatem meam.
     non te pro his curasse rebus nequid aegre esset mihi!
     SO. non mea opera neque pol culpa evenit. LA. immo maxume.
     sola hic fuisti; in te omnis haeret culpa sola, Sostrata.
230   quae hic erant curares, quom ego vos curis solvi ceteris.

SOSTRATA:(205)Oh dear! What I'm being blamed for now I really can't imagine.

LACHES: *(Sarcastically)* Huh! Can't you?

SOSTRATA: No, Laches dear, I can't, so heaven help me and grant that we live out our lives together.

LACHES: Heaven forbid!

SOSTRATA: One day you'll find out your accusations against me are undeserved, I'm sure of it.

LACHES: Undeserved? Are there any words sufficient to describe you for what you've done? **(210)** You're bringing disgrace on me *and* yourself *and* the family, as well as storing up grief for our son, not to mention making his in-laws our enemies instead of our friends, and after they thought him a fit person to entrust their daughter to. But single-handed *you* came on the scene to upset all this with your shameless behaviour!

SOSTRATA: I did?

LACHES: *(Shouting)* Yes you, woman. You think I'm made of stone right through, not flesh and blood. **(215)** Or do you women think that because I'm often at the farm I don't know how each of you passes the time here? I'm far better informed of what goes on here than in the country where I usually am, precisely because my reputation among others depends on how *you people* behave at home. Some time ago in fact I heard Philumena had taken a dislike to you, **(220)** and really it's hardly surprising. Actually it would be more surprising if she hadn't, but I didn't believe it extended to a hatred of the whole household as well! If I had known, *she* would have stayed and *you* would have been sent packing. *(Reduces his anger to a tone of appeal)* But Sostrata, can't you realise how undeserved this distress you're causing me is? I went off to live on the farm out of consideration for you and to look after the estate **(225)** so that our income could meet your expenses and maintain your life of leisure. I made no concessions to hard work, even when it went beyond what was fair and right at my time of life. *(Becoming heated again)* But in return *you* didn't care about sparing *me* any worries!

SOSTRATA: But it's not my doing, not my fault this has happened.

LACHES: Oh yes it is, very much so. You were here alone, so all the blame rests on you alone, Sostrata. **(230)** I freed you from all other responsibilities, so you

cum puella anum suscepisse inimicitias non pudet?

illius dices culpa factum? SO. haud equidem dico, mi Lache.

LA. gaudeo, ita me di ament, gnati causa; nam de te quidem

satis scio peccando detrimenti nil fieri potest.

235   SO. qui scis an ea causa, mi vir, me odisse adsimulaverit

ut cum matre plus una esset? LA. quid ais? non signi hoc sat est,

quod heri nemo voluit visentem ad eam te intro admittere?

SO. enim lassam oppido tum esse aibant; eo ad eam non admissa sum.

LA. tuos esse ego illi mores morbum mage quam ullam aliam rem

arbitror,

240   et merito adeo; nam vostrarum nullast quin gnatum velit

ducere uxorem, et quae vobis placitast condicio datur.

ubi duxere inpulsu vostro, vostro inpulsu easdem exigunt.

(II ii) **Phidippus Laches Sostrata**

PH. Etsi scio ego, Philumena, meum ius esse ut te cogam

quae ego imperem facere, ego tamen patrio animo victus faciam

245   ut tibi concedam neque tuae lubidini advorsabor.

LA. atque eccum Phidippum optume video; hinc iam scibo hoc quid sit.

Phidippe, etsi ego meis me omnibus scio esse adprime obsequentem,

sed non adeo ut mea facilitas corrumpat illorum animos;

quod tu si idem faceres, magis in rem et vostram et nostram id esset.

250   nunc video in illarum potestate esse te. PH. heia vero?

LA. adii te heri de filia; ut veni, itidem incertum amisti.

haud ita decet, si perpetuam hanc vis esse adfinitatem,

celare te iras. siquid est peccatum a nobis profer:

aut ea refellendo aut purgando vobis corrigemus

should have looked after things here. Aren't you ashamed at having started a quarrel with a girl at your age? Are you going to say it was *her* fault?

SOSTRATA: No, Laches dear, I'm not saying that.

LACHES: I'm glad, by heaven - for our son's sake. As for you, I'm perfectly well aware that you've nothing to lose by behaving badly. **(235)**

SOSTRATA: But Laches, how do you know she didn't pretend to dislike me just so she could spend more time with her mother?

LACHES: What? Isn't it enough proof that no one would let you in when you tried to visit her yesterday?

SOSTRATA: No. They said she was quite worn out just then: that's why they wouldn't let me in.

LACHES: I think her indisposition had more to do with *your* character than anything else, **(240)** and small wonder. There isn't one of you women that doesn't want her son to get married, and the match you decide on is the one that's arranged. Then, once you've pressured them into taking a wife, you pressure them into getting rid of them.

(From the third door Phidippus appears, addressing his daughter inside)

(II ii)

PHIDIPPUS: *(Mildly)* I'm well aware I have the right to force you into carrying out my instructions, Philumena; but my fatherly affection makes me **(245)** give in to you and not stand in the way of your whims.

LACHES: Ah, here's Phidippus, just at the right time. *(Phidippus turns, sees Laches and approaches)* I'll find out from him what all this is about. Phidippus, I know I'm indulgent in the extreme towards all the members of my family, but not to the extent of allowing my good nature to ruin their characters. If you did the same, it'd be to the advantage of us both. **(250)** As it is, I see you're under the thumb of your womenfolk.

PHIDIPPUS: *(Taken aback)* Is that so?

LACHES: I called on you yesterday about your daughter, and you sent me away as mystified as when I came. If you want this marriage alliance between us to last, it really will not do to keep the cause of your anger secret. If we have done anything wrong, tell us; we'll either disprove it or apologise to you and make

255   te iudice ipso. sin east causa retinendi apud vos
      quia aegrast, te mihi iniuriam facere arbitror, Phidippe,
      si metuis satis ut meae domi curetur diligenter.
      at ita me di ament, haud tibi hoc concedo - etsi illi pater es -
      ut tu illam salvam mage velis quam ego - id adeo gnati causa,
260   quem ego intellexi illam haud minus quam se ipsum magni facere.
      neque adeo clam me est quam esse eum graviter laturum credam,
      hoc si rescierit; eo domum studeo haec prius quam ille redeat.
      PH. Laches, et diligentiam vostram et benignitatem
      novi, et quae dicis omnia esse ut dicis animum induco,
265   et te hoc mihi cupio credere: illam ad vos redire studeo
      si facere possim ullo modo. **LA**. quae res te id facere prohibet?
      eho num quidnam accusat virum? **PH**. minime; nam postquam attendi
      magis et vi coepi cogere ut rediret, sancte adiurat
      non posse apud vos Pamphilo se absente perdurare.
270   aliud fortasse aliis viti est: ego sum animo leni natus;
      non possum advorsari meis. **LA**. em, Sostrata. **SO**. heu me miseram!
      LA. certumne est istuc? **PH**. nunc quidem ut videtur; sed numquid vis?
      nam est quod me transire ad forum iam oportet. **LA**. eo tecum una.

(II iii) Sostrata

      Edepol ne nos sumus inique aeque omnes invisae viris
275   propter paucas, quae omnes faciunt dignae ut videamur malo.
      nam ita me di ament, quod me accusat nunc vir, sum extra noxiam.
      sed non facile est expurgatu: ita animum induxerunt socrus
      omnis esse iniquas; haud pol mequidem; nam numquam secus

whatever amends **(255)** you yourself see fit. If on the other hand the reason for keeping the girl at your place is because she's ill, I take it as an insult on your part, if you're afraid she won't be sufficiently well looked after in my house. Heavens above! Even if you are her father, I can't have you thinking *you* care for her welfare more than *I* do; not least for my son's sake, **(260)** knowing as I do that he values her no less dearly than himself. What's more, I'm only too well aware of how upset I think he'll be if he finds out about it. That's why I'm anxious for her to return home before *he* does.

PHIDIPPUS: *(With a tone of reassurance)* Laches, I have no doubts about your care and kindness, and I'm sure everything you say is as you say. **(265)** In turn I want you to believe me when I say that I'm anxious for her to return to you if I can possibly bring it about.

LACHES: What's stopping you? Come now, she's not making any complaint against her husband is she?

PHIDIPPUS: Not in the least. When I pressed the matter and began insisting that she return, she swore a solemn oath that she couldn't stand living in your house while Pamphilus was away. **(270)** We all have our faults, one way or another. Personally I was born with a mild disposition - I just can't go against my family.

LACHES: *(Turns to his wife)* There you are, Sostrata.

SOSTRATA: Oh dear, I feel so unhappy.

LACHES: *(To Phidippus)* Is that decision final?

PHIDIPPUS: For the time being at least, so it would seem. Now, if there's nothing else, there's some business I have to go to that forum about right now.

LACHES: I'll come with you. *(The old men ⸱ ⸱t right, leaving Sostrata alone)*
(II iii)

SOSTRATA: Oh dear, it really is unfair how we women are all alike in being hated by our husbands - **(275)** just because of a few whose behaviour makes us all seem worthy of being treated badly. So heaven help me - I'm innocent of my husband's accusations, but clearing oneself is no easy matter - people take it for granted that all mothers-in-law are unkind. In my case, though, it just isn't so. I've

habui illam ac si ex me esset gnata, nec qui hoc mi eveniat scio;
280   nisi pol filium multimodis iam exspecto ut redeat domum.

(III i) **Pamphilus Parmeno (Myrrina)**

PAM. Nemini plura acerba credo esse ex amore homini umquam oblata
quam mi. heu me infelicem! hancin ego vitam parsi perdere!
hacin causa ego eram tanto opere cupidus redeundi domum! hui,
quanto fuerat praestabilius ubivis gentium agere aetatem
285   quam huc redire atque haec ita esse miserum me resciscere!
nam nos omnes quibus est alicunde aliquis obiectus labos,
omne quod est interea tempus prius quam id rescitumst lucrost.
PAR. at sic citius qui te expedias his aerumnis reperias.
si non rediisses, haec irae factae essent multo ampliores.
290   sed nunc adventum tuom ambas, Pamphile, scio reverituras:
rem cognosces, iram expedies, rursum in gratiam restitues.
levia sunt quae tu pergravia esse in animum induxti tuom.
PAM. quid consolare me? an quisquam usquam gentiumst aeque miser?
prius quam hanc uxorem duxi, habebam alibi animum amori deditum;
295   tamen numquam ausus sum recusare eam quam mi obtrudit pater.
iam in hac re, ut taceam, quoivis facile scitust quam fuerim miser.
vix me illim abstraxi atque inpeditum in ea expedivi animum meum,
vixque huc contuleram: em, nova res ortast porro ab hac quae me
    abstrahat.
tum matrem ex ea re me aut uxorem in culpa inventurum arbitror;
300   quod quom ita esse invenero, quid restat nisi porro ut fiam miser?
nam matris ferre iniurias me, Parmeno, pietas iubet;
tum uxori obnoxius sum: ita olim suo me ingenio pertulit,
tot meas iniurias quae numquam in ullo patefecit loco.

never treated her any differently than if she were my own daughter and I simply can't think how this could happen to me. (280) Oh, how very much I'm longing for my son to return home.

(Withdraws into her house. After a few moments Pamphilus and Parmeno enter from the left in conversation)

(III i)

PAMPHILUS: I don't think anyone has ever had more bitter experiences inflicted on him through love than I have. Just my rotten luck! Is this what I strove to keep myself alive for? Was it for this I was so anxious to return home? Huh, I'd have been far better off living anywhere on earth (285) than come back here and find to my dismay that things are in this state! All of us who have trouble lying in wait for us from one source or another, well, all the time spent before we come to it is pure gain.

PARMENO: *(Trying to see things in a better light)* But this way you can find a quicker escape from these problems. If you hadn't returned, this resentment would have become much more serious. (290) As it is, Pamphilus, I'm certain your arrival will bring them both to their senses. You'll discover the facts, settle their quarrel, and make them friends again. The things you've convinced yourself are desperately serious are just trifles.

PAMPHILUS: Why try to comfort me? Is there a soul alive anywhere who's as unhappy? Before I married the girl my heart was pledged in love elsewhere, (295) but I never dared refuse the wife my father foisted on me. In a situation like that it must be clear to anyone how unhappy I was, without being told by me. I'd barely extricated myself from that affair and freed my emotions from their entanglement with her, I'd just transferred them to my wife here when - lo and behold - something new cropped up to take me away from *her* too. What's more, I expect I'll find either my mother or my wife is to blame as a result, (300) and when I find that is the case, what's left for me but further misery? Duty calls me to put up with my mother's faults, Parmeno, but then again I do owe my wife something. Because of her good nature she put up with me in the early days and never breathed so much as a word about all my unkindnesses. But it must have been

sed magnum nescioquid necessest evenisse, Parmeno,

305 unde ira inter eas intercessit quae tam permansit diu.

PAR. haud quidem hercle: parvom. si vis vero veram rationem exsequi,

non maxumas quae maxumae sunt interdum irae iniurias

faciunt; nam saepe est quibus in rebus alius ne iratus quidem est,

quom de eadem causast iracundus factus inimicissimus.

310 pueri inter sese quam pro levibus noxiis iras gerunt -

quapropter? quia enim qui eos gubernat animus eum infirmum gerunt.

itidem illae mulieres sunt ferme ut pueri levi sententia.

fortasse unum aliquod verbum inter eas iram hanc concivisse.

PAM. abi, Parmeno, intro ac me venisse nuntia. **PAR**. hem quid hoc est?

      PAM. tace.

315 trepidari sentio et cursari rursum prorsum. **PAR**. agedum, ad fores

accedo propius. em, sensistin? **PAM**. noli fabularier.

pro Iuppiter, clamorem audivi! **PAR**. tute loqueris, me vetas.

MY.(*intus*) tace obsecro, mea gnata. **PAM**. matris vox visast

      Philumenae.

nullus sum! **PAR**. quidum? **PAM**. perii! **PAR**. quam ob rem?

      PAM. nescioquod magnum malum

320 profecto, Parmeno, me celant. **PAR**. uxorem Philumenam

pavitare nescioquid dixerunt. id si forte est nescio.

PAM. interii! quor mihi id non dixti? **PAR**. quia non poteram una

      omnia.

something serious that happened, Parmeno, **(305)** to have produced a state of resentment between them that's lasted so long.

PARMENO: *(Reassuringly)* Good Lord no, a minor matter. If you care to consider it logically, the greatest quarrels don't always presuppose the greatest wrongs. It's often the case that where one man doesn't even raise an eyebrow at a situation, a hot-tempered individual in the same situation becomes the deadliest of enemies. **(310)** Children bear grudges against one another over even the most minor offences, and why? - because the temperaments they're governed by aren't fully developed. Those women too are pretty much like children - fickle-minded. It may well be that a single word has provoked this resentment between them.

PAMPHILUS: Go inside then, Parmeno, and tell them I've arrived. *(Parmeno starts towards Phidippus' house but is halted by noises coming from inside)*

PARMENO: Hello, what's that?

PAMPHILUS: *(Impatiently)* Quiet. **(315)** I can hear a commotion and people running backwards and forwards.

PARMENO: Come on. I'll get closer to the door. *(More noises from inside)* There! Did you hear that?

PAMPHILUS: *(With greater irritation)* Oh, do be quiet. *(A cry within. Pamphilus recoils in horror)* God! That was a cry I heard.

PARMENO: *(Hurt)* You talk away and tell me not to.

MYRRINA: *(Inside)* Hush daughter, please.

PAMPHILUS: That sounded like Philumena's mother. This is awful!

PARMENO: How come?

PAMPHILUS: *(Ignoring Parmeno's question)* Disaster!

PARMENO: Why?

PAMPHILUS: It's something really dreadful **(320)** they're hiding from me, Parmeno.

PARMENO: *(Weakly and apologetically)* They did say your wife Philumena had some kind of fever. I don't know if that's what this is.

PAMPHILUS: Oh no! Why didn't you tell me?

PARMENO: I couldn't tell you everything at once.

PAM. quid morbi est? **PAR.** nescio. **PAM.** quid? nemon medicum
adduxit? **PAR.** nescio.

PAM. cesso hinc ire intro ut hoc quam primum, quidquid est, certo
sciam?

325 quonam modo, Philumena mea, nunc te offendam adfectam?
nam si periclum ullum in te inest, perisse me una haud dubiumst.

PAR. non usus factost mihi nunc hunc intro sequi;
nam invisos omnis nos esse illis sentio:
heri nemo voluit Sostratam intro admittere.

330 si forte morbus amplior factus siet,
quod sane nolim, maxume eri causa mei,
servom ilico introisse dicent Sostratae,
aliquid tulisse comminiscentur mali
capiti atque aetati illorum, morbus qui auctu' sit.

335 era in crimen veniet, ego vero in magnum malum.

(III ii) Sostrata Parmeno Pamphilus

SO. Nescioquid iamdudum audio hic tumultuari misera.
male metuo ne Philumenae mage morbus adgravescat;
quod te, Aesculapi, et te, Salus, nequid sit huius oro.
nunc ad eam visam. **PAR.** heus Sostrata! **SO.** hem. **PAR.** iterum istinc
excludere.

340 **SO.** ehem Parmeno, tun hic eras? perii, quid faciam misera?
non visam uxorem Pamphili, quom in proxumo hic sit aegra?
PAR. non visas? ne mittas quidem visendi causa quemquam.
nam qui amat quoi odio ipsus est, bis facere stulte duco:
laborem inanem ipsus capit et illi molestiam adfert.

345 tum filius tuos intro iit videre, ut venit, quid agat.

PAMPHILUS: What's the matter with her?

PARMENO: I don't know.

PAMPHILUS: Well, hasn't anyone sent for a doctor?

PARMENO: I don't know.

PAMPHILUS: Then why am I wasting time out here instead of going straight inside and finding out exactly what this is all about? *(Turns to rush inside)* **(325)** Oh Philumena darling, what state will I find you in? If you're in any danger, I've no choice but to die with you. *(Dashes into Phidippus' house)*

PARMENO: No point my going in after him now. I can see we're all hated by these people - yesterday no one would let Sostrata in. **(330)** If the illness somehow takes a turn for the worse - something I very much hope doesn't happen, especially for my master's sake - they'll straight away say a servant of Sostrata's has been in and pretend he's brought something with him that's harmful to the lives and well-being of them all, something that's caused the illness to get worse. **(335)** Mistress will then get the blame, and I'll be in big trouble.

(From Laches' house Sostrata re-emerges in a state of apprehension)
(III ii)

SOSTRATA: Oh dear, I've been hearing sounds of commotion next door for some time now. I'm very much afraid Philumena's illness is getting worse. *(Raises her hands to heaven)* Please, Aesculapius, and you too goddess of health, don't let it be anything like that. I'll go and see her. *(Moves towards Phidippus' door)*

PARMENO: *(Interrupting)* Er, Sostrata!

SOSTRATA: *(Surprised and looking round)* What?

PARMENO: You'll be refused entry again. **(340)**

SOSTRATA: *(Catches sight of Parmeno)* Ah, Parmeno, is that you? Oh dear, this is awful; what am I to do? Can't I even go and see Pamphilus' wife when she's lying ill right next door here?

PARMENO: Not go and see her? Why, you shouldn't even send anyone to see her! To love someone who finds you objectionable I think is being doubly stupid: wasted effort on your own part and annoyance for the other side. **(345)** In any case, as soon as your son arrived he went in to see how she's doing.

SO. quid ais? an venit Pamphilus? **PAR.** venit. **SO.** dis gratiam habeo.

hem, istoc verbo animus mihi redit et cura ex corde excessit.

PAR. iam ea te causa maxume nunc hoc intro ire nolo;

nam si remittent quidpiam Philumenae dolores,

350 omnem rem narrabit, scio, continuo sola soli

quae inter vos intervenerit, unde ortumst initium irae.

atque eccum video ipsum egredi; quam tristist! **SO.** o mi gnate!

PAM. mea mater, salve. **SO.** gaudeo venisse salvom. salvan

Philumenast? **PAM.** meliusculast. **SO.** utinam istuc ita di faxint!

355 quid tu igitur lacrumas? aut quid es tam tristis? **PAM.** recte mater.

SO. quid fuit tumulti? dic mihi: an dolor repente invasit?

PAM. ita factumst. **SO.** quid morbi est? **PAM.** febris. **SO.** cotidiana?

PAM. ita aiunt.

i sodes intro, consequar iam te, mea mater. **SO.** fiat.

PAM. tu pueris curre, Parmeno, obviam atque is onera adiuta.

360 **PAR.** quid? non sciunt ipsi viam domum qua veniant? **PAM.** cessas?

SOSTRATA: *(In a tone of astonished delight)* What's that you're saying? Is Pamphilus back?

PARMENO: Yes.

SOSTRATA: Thank God! Well, that puts heart back in me and takes a weight off my mind.

PARMENO: And that's precisely the reason I don't want you going inside just now. If Philumena's pain gets any better, **(350)** as soon as they're alone together she'll tell him everything that came between you and how her resentment arose in the first place. I'm sure of it. *(Pamphilus appears at Phidippus' door clearly shaken and in tears)* And here he is coming out. How dejected he looks!

SOSTRATA: Pamphilus!

PAMPHILUS: *(Putting on a brave face)* Hello, mother.

SOSTRATA: I'm glad you've got back safely. Is all well with Philumena?

PAMPHILUS: She's a little better.

SOSTRATA: Pray God it's so. **(355)** But why then are you crying? Why are you looking so dejected?

PAMPHILUS: It's all right, mother.

SOSTRATA: Then what was all the commotion about? Tell me - did she have a sudden attack of pain?

PAMPHILUS: *(Latching on to her suggested explanation)* Yes, that's what it was.

SOSTRATA: What's the matter with her?

PAMPHILUS: A fever.

SOSTRATA: Nothing serious?

PAMPHILUS: So they say, but, please mother, go back indoors and I'll join you presently.

SOSTRATA: Very well. *(Exits indoors once again)*

PAMPHILUS: Parmeno, run and meet the slaves and help them with the luggage. **(360)**

PARMENO: *(Indignantly)* What! Don't they know the way home themselves?

PAMPHILUS: *(Rounds on the slave angrily)* You not gone yet? *(Parmeno leaves grudgingly towards the harbour; Pamphilus, now alone, turns to review the situation)*

(III iii) **Pamphilus**

Nequeo mearum rerum initium ullum invenire idoneum
unde exordiar narrare quae necopinanti accidunt,
partim quae perspexi hisce oculis, partim quae accepi auribus;
qua me propter exanimatum citius eduxi foras.
365   nam modo intro me ut corripui timidus, alio suspicans
morbo me visurum adfectam ac sensi esse uxorem: ei mihi!
postquam me aspexere ancillae advenisse, ilico omnes simul
laetae exclamant "venit", id quod me repente aspexerant.
sed continuo voltum earum sensi inmutari omnium,
370   quia tam incommode illic fors obtulerat adventum meum.
una illarum interea propere praecucurrit nuntians
me venisse; ego eius videndi cupidus recta consequor.
postquam intro adveni, extemplo eius morbum cognovi miser;
nam neque ut celari posset tempus spatium ullum dabat,
375   neque voce alia ac res monebat ipsa poterat conqueri.
postquam aspexi, "o facinus indignum" inquam et corripui ilico
me inde lacrumans, incredibili re atque atroci percitus.
mater consequitur; iam ut limen exirem, ad genua accidit
lacrumans misera; miseritumst. profecto hoc sic est, ut puto:
380   omnibus nobis ut res dant sese ita magni atque humiles sumus.
hanc habere orationem mecum principio institit:
"o mi Pamphile, abs te quam ob rem haec abierit causam vides;
nam vitiumst oblatum virgini olim a nescioquo inprobo.
nunc huc confugit te atque alios partum ut celaret suom."
385   sed quom orata huius reminiscor nequeo quin lacrumem miser.
"quaeque fors fortunast" inquit "nobis quae te hodie obtulit,
per eam te obsecramus ambae, si ius si fas est, uti
advorsa eius per te tecta tacitaque apud omnis sient.
si umquam erga te animo esse amico sensisti eam, mi Pamphile,
390   sine labore hanc gratiam te uti sibi des pro illa nunc rogat.

(III iii)

      Finding a suitable starting point from which to begin describing the things that are happening when I least expect them is quite beyond me. Some of them I've seen with my own eyes; others I've heard. It's because of them I've come rushing out in this confused state. **(365)** When I dashed inside just now full of apprehension, I was expecting to see my wife suffering from quite a different ailment from the one I found. *(Gasps in despair)* Oh God! When the maids saw I'd arrived, straight away they were all smiles and cried out with one voice: "He's here" - smiles because they'd not been expecting to see me. The next moment though I saw all their faces change - **(370)** chance had evidently arranged my arrival there at precisely the wrong moment. Then one of them raced on ahead to report my arrival. I was anxious to see my wife and followed right after her, but when I got inside, I could see straight away what was wrong with her - worse luck. Circumstances didn't give any opportunity for covering it up, **(375)** and the only cries she herself could utter were what her condition dictated. I took one look, burst out with "Monstrous outrage!" and immediately dashed off in tears, overwhelmed by this unbelievable and dreadful turn of events. Her mother came after me, and just as I was going out through the door, the poor woman fell to her knees in tears. It was a pitiful sight. The fact is, I suppose, **(380)** we're all humble or proud as circumstances permit. First of all this is how she began: "Oh Pamphilus, you see the reason why she left your home. She was assaulted by some reprobate before her marriage, and now she's taken refuge here in order to conceal the birth from you and from everyone else". **(385)** But when I think of her entreaties, I can't help bursting into tears of anguish. She went on: "Whatever chance has brought you to us today, we both implore you by it, if the laws of God and man allow, to keep her troubles hidden and secret from everyone. Oh Pamphilus, if you have ever felt her kindness towards you, **(390)** she begs you now to grant her this favour in return - it won't cost you anything. But as for taking her

ceterum de redducenda id facias quod in rem sit tuam.
parturire eam nec gravidam esse ex te solus consciu's;
nam aiunt tecum post duobus concubuisse mensibus;
tum, postquam ad te venit, mensis agitur hic iam septimus.
395　quod te scire ipsa indicat res. nunc si potis est, Pamphile,
maxume volo doque operam ut clam partus eveniat patrem
atque adeo omnis. sed si id fieri non potest quin sentiant,
dicam abortum esse. scio nemini aliter suspectum fore
quin, quod veri similest, ex te recte eum natum putent.
400　continuo exponetur; hic tibi nil est quicquam incommodi,
et illi miserae indigne factam iniuriam contexeris."
pollicitus sum et servare in eo certumst quod dixi fidem.
nam de redducenda, id vero ne utiquam honestum esse arbitror
nec faciam, etsi amor me graviter consuetudoque eius tenet.
405　lacrumo quae posthac futurast vita quom in mentem venit
solitudoque. o fortuna, ut numquam perpetuo es data!
sed iam prior amor me ad hanc rem exercitatum reddidit,
quem ego tum consilio missum feci; idem huc operam dabo.
adest Parmeno cum pueris. hunc minimest opus
410　in hac re adesse; nam olim soli credidi
ea me abstinuisse in principio quom datast.
vereor, si clamorem eius hic crebro exaudiat,
ne parturire intellegat. aliquo mihist
hinc ablegandus dum parit Philumena.

(III iv) **Parmeno Sosia Pamphilus**

415　**PAR.** Ain tu tibi hoc incommodum evenisse iter?
　　SOS. non hercle verbis, Parmeno, dici potest
　　tantum quam re ipsa navigare incommodumst.

back, you must do as you see fit. No one else but you knows that she's in labour and that you're not the father: I'm told it was two months before she slept with you, and it's now seven months since she came to you. **(395)** But then events themselves show you know this. Now, what I very much want and what I'm aiming at, Pamphilus, is for the birth to take place without her father or indeed anyone else getting to know, if that's at all possible. But if we can't avoid them finding out about it, I'll say there's been a miscarriage. I'm certain no one will suspect otherwise; no one but will think the child is really yours, which is how it seems. **(400)** It'll exposed straight away. There'll be no problems for yourself in any of this, and you'll have concealed the shameful wrong done to the poor girl." I gave my promise and I'm determined to keep my word on the undertaking I gave. As for taking her back, I don't think that's at all the right thing to do, and I won't do it, even though the feelings of love and companionship I have for her exert a strong hold on me. **(405)** Tears well up when I think of life in the future and the loneliness. Oh Fortune, how short-lived is our enjoyment of you! *(Wipes away the tears and steels himself)* My old love affair though - the one I deliberately gave up - that's trained me well for this. I'll apply myself the same way in the present case. *(Enter Parmeno with a party of slaves loaded with baggage)* Here's Parmeno with the slaves: he's the last person who needs **(410)** to be involved in this. He's the only one I confided in at the time that I didn't touch my wife when we were first married. If he hears her repeated cries, I'm afraid he'll realise she's in labour. I'll have to send him off somewhere till Philumena gives birth.

(Parmeno, deep in conversation with one of the slaves, fails to notice his young master on the other side of the stage) **(415)**

(III iv)

PARMENO: You mean this voyage of yours turned out an unpleasant experience?
SOSIA: Why, words can't express how unpleasant travel by boat actually is, Parmeno.

PAR. itan est? **SOS.** o fortunate, nescis quid mali
praeterieris qui numquam es ingressus mare.
420 nam alias ut mittam miserias, unam hanc vide:
dies triginta aut plus eo in navi fui,
quom interea semper mortem exspectabam miser;
ita usque advorsa tempestate usi sumus.
PAR. odiosum. **SOS.** haud clam me est. denique hercle aufugerim
425 potius quam redeam, si eo mihi redeundum sciam.
PAR. olim quidem te causae inpellebant leves
quod nunc minitare facere ut faceres, Sosia.
sed Pamphilum ipsum video stare ante ostium.
ite intro; ego hunc adibo, siquid me velit.
430 ere, etiam tu hic stas? **PAM.** et quidem te exspecto. **PAR.** quid est?
PAM. in arcem transcurso opus est. **PAR.** quoi homini? **PAM.** tibi.
PAR. in arcem? quid eo? **PAM.** Callidemidem hospitem
Myconium, qui mecum una vectust, conveni.
PAR. perii. vovisse hunc dicam, si salvos domum
435 redisset umquam, ut me ambulando rumperet?
PAM. quid cessas? **PAR.** quid vis dicam? an conveniam modo?
PAM. immo quod constitui me hodie conventurum eum,
non posse, ne me frustra illi exspectet. vola.
PAR. at non novi hominis faciem. **PAM.** at faciam ut noveris:
440 magnus, rubicundus, crispus, crassus, caesius,
cadaverosa facie. **PAR.** di illum perduint!
quid si non veniet? maneamne usque ad vesperum?

PARMENO: Really?

SOSIA: You're lucky - you don't know what trouble you've escaped in never having been to sea. **(420)** Apart from all the other miseries, just consider this one example: thirty days or more I was on board and there wasn't a moment I wasn't constantly expecting to die. That's how bad the weather was from start to finish.

PARMENO: Dreadful!

SOSIA: Don't I know it! In fact, I'd run away **(425)** rather than come back if I knew I had to go back there again.

PARMENO: Well, it certainly didn't take much in the past to get you doing what you're now threatening, Sosia. *(Sees Pamphilus)* But there's Pamphilus standing in front of the door. Off you go inside; I'll go to him and see if he wants me for anything. *(Sosia and the other slaves disappear into Laches' house)* **(430)** You still standing here, master?

PAMPHILUS: Yes, it's you I'm waiting for.

PARMENO: *(Suspiciously)* What for?

PAMPHILUS: It's imperative someone runs up to the Citadel.

PARMENO: Imperative for whom?

PAMPHILUS: You.

PARMENO: The Citadel? Why there?

PAMPHILUS: Find Callidemides, the man I stayed with on Myconos and who took ship with me.

PARMENO: *(Aside)* Damn! Do I take it he vowed **(435)** to rupture me with all this toing and froing if ever he got home safely?

PAMPHILUS: What are you hanging around for?

PARMENO: What do you want me to say? Or am I just to find him?

PAMPHILUS: No, tell him that as regards my appointment to meet him today, I can't make it; so he needn't waste his time waiting for me there. Now fly!

PARMENO: *(Puzzled)* But I don't know what the man looks like.

PAMPHILUS: Then I'll make sure you do know him - **(440)** big chap, ruddy complexion, curly hair, fat, grey eyes, face like a corpse.

PARMENO: Good grief! What if he doesn't come? Should I hang around till nightfall?

PAM. maneto; curre. PAR. non queo; ita defessu' sum.
PAM. ille abiit. quid agam infelix? prorsus nescio
445   quo pacto hoc celem quod me oravit Myrrina,
suae gnatae partum; nam me miseret mulieris.
quod potero faciam, tamen ut pietatem colam;
nam me parenti potius quam amori obsequi
oportet. attat eccum Phidippum et patrem
450   video; horsum pergunt. quid dicam hisce incertu' sum.

(III v) Laches Phidippus Pamphilus

LA. Dixtin dudum illam dixisse se exspectare filium?
PH. factum. LA. venisse aiunt; redeat. PAM. causam quam dicam patri
quam ob rem non reducam nescio. LA. quem ego hic audivi loqui?
PAM. certum offirmare est viam me quam decrevi persequi.
455   LA. ipsus est de quo hoc agebam tecum. PAM. salve, mi pater.
LA. gnate mi, salve. PH. bene factum te advenisse, Pamphile,
atque adeo, id quod maxumumst, salvom atque validum. PAM. creditur.
LA. advenis modo? PAM. admodum. LA. cedo, quid reliquit Phania,
consobrinus noster? PAM. sane hercle homo voluptati obsequens
460   fuit dum vixit et qui sic sunt haud multum heredem iuvant;
sibi vero hanc laudem relinquont: "vixit, dum vixit, bene."
LA. tum tu igitur nil attulisti plus una hac sententia?

PAMPHILUS: Yes, do that. Now run!

PARMENO: I can't; I'm so tired. *(Trails off to the right)*

PAMPHILUS: He's gone. Oh dear, what am I to do? I really don't know **(445)** how I'm to keep secret what Myrrina begged me to - the fact that her daughter's having a baby - much as I'd like to since I'm sorry for the woman. I'll do what I can as far as my duty as a son allows. After all I ought to put my mother before my love. *(Enter Laches and Phidippus from the right)* Oh! There's Phidippus and my father. **(450)** They're coming this way. What to tell them I've really no idea.

(III v)

LACHES: Didn't you say just now she claimed she was waiting for my son?

PHIDIPPUS: That's right.

LACHES: I'm told he's arrived, so she can come back.

PAMPHILUS: *(Aside)* What reason I can give my father for not taking her back I just don't know.

LACHES: *(Looks round)* Who's that I hear talking?

PAMPHILUS: *(Aside)* I'm determined to stick to the course I've decided to follow. **(455)**

LACHES: *(Sees Pamphilus)* The very man I was on to you about.

PAMPHILUS: Hello, father.

LACHES: Welcome back, my boy!

PHIDIPPUS: It's good to have you back, Pamphilus, and, what's more important, safe and sound.

PAMPHILUS: Thank you.

LACHES: Just got back?

PAMPHILUS: Yes, just now.

LACHES: *(Eagerly)* Well, out with it. What did our cousin Phania leave?

PAMPHILUS: To tell the truth, he was a man very much given over to pleasure **(460)** while he was alive, and people like that don't do a lot for their heirs. For themselves, though, they leave behind the epitaph: "His was a good life while it lasted".

LACHES: So all you've brought back is this one saying?

PAM. quidquid est id quod reliquit, profuit. LA. immo obfuit;
nam illum vivom et salvom vellem. PH. inpune optare istuc licet;
465 ill' revivescet iam numquam, et tamen utrum malis scio.
LA. heri Philumenam ad se accersi hic iussit. dic iussisse te.
PH. noli fodere. iussi. LA. sed eam iam remittet. PH. scilicet.
PAM. omnem rem scio ut sit gesta; adveniens audivi modo.
LA. at istos invidos di perdant qui haec lubenter nuntiant.
470 PAM. ego me scio cavisse ne ulla merito contumelia
fieri a vobis posset; idque si nunc memorare hic velim
quam fideli animo et benigno in illam et clementi fui,
vere possum, ni te ex ipsa haec mage velim resciscere;
namque eo pacto maxume apud te meo erit ingenio fides.
475 quom illa, quae nunc in me iniquast, aequa de me dixerit.
neque mea culpa hoc discidium evenisse, id testor deos.
sed quando sese esse indignam deputat matri meae
quae concedat cuiusque mores toleret sua modestia,
neque alio pacto componi potest inter eas gratia,
480 segreganda aut mater a me est, Phidippe, aut Philumena.
nunc me pietas matris potius commodum suadet sequi.
LA. Pamphile, haud invito ad auris sermo mi accessit tuos,
quom te postputasse omnis res prae parente intellego;
verum vide ne inpulsus ira prave insistas, Pamphile.
485 PAM. quibus iris pulsus nunc in illam iniquo' sim
quae numquam quicquam erga me commeritast, pater,
quod nollem, et saepe quod vellem meritam scio?

PAMPHILUS: Whatever his estate amounts to, it's our profit.

LACHES: On the contrary, our loss. I'd rather he were alive and well.

PHIDIPPUS: That's a wish won't cost you anything. (**465**) *He*'ll never come back to life again, and yet I know which you'd prefer.

LACHES: Yesterday Phidippus here gave instructions for Philumena to be fetched over to his place. *(Nudges Phidippus in the ribs with his elbow)* Say you gave instructions.

PHIDIPPUS: *(To Laches)* Don't dig - *(To Pamphilus)* I gave instructions.

LACHES: But now he'll send her back.

PHIDIPPUS: Of course.

PAMPHILUS: I know exactly how things stand. I was told just now when I arrived.

LACHES: *(Annoyed)* Damn those mischief-makers who enjoy spreading gossip like that. (**470**)

PAMPHILUS: *(Adopts a moralistic tone)* Phidippus, I'm conscious of having taken care not to deserve any reproach from your family, and if I wanted to mention here and now how faithful, kind and forbearing I've been towards Philumena, I could certainly do so, though I'd prefer you to learn this from her own lips. That way you're most likely to have confidence in my character - (**475**) when the wife who currently does me wrong speaks fairly of me. I call upon the gods to witness that this break between us hasn't come about through any fault of mine. But since she considers it beneath her dignity to give way to my mother and to put up with her ways by exercising some self-control, and since there's no other way that good relations can be established between them, (**480**) then, Phidippus, I must give up either my mother or Philumena. Under the circumstances my sense of duty persuades me to put my mother's interests first.

LACHES: What you say, Pamphilus, isn't unwelcome to my ears, since it's clear to me you've put your mother before all else, but be careful you're not being driven into taking a wrong course of action by feelings of resentment. (**485**)

PAMPHILUS: What feelings of resentment could drive me into being hurtful to her when she's never been guilty of any act towards me I might disapprove of, and when I know she's often behaved exactly as I wanted? I love her and praise her; I

amoque et laudo et vehementer desidero;

nam fuisse erga me miro ingenio expertu' sum;

490   illique exopto ut relicuam vitam exigat

cum eo viro me qui sit fortunatior,

quandoquidem illam a me distrahit necessitas.

PH. tibi id in manust ne fiat. **LA.** si sanus sies...

iube illam redire. **PAM.** non est consilium, pater;

495   matris servibo commodis. **LA.** quo abis? mane

mane, inquam; quo abis? **PH.** quae haec est pertinacia?

LA. dixin, Phidippe, hanc rem aegre laturum esse eum?

quam ob rem te orabam filiam ut remitteres.

PH. non credidi edepol adeo inhumanum fore.

500   ita nunc is sibi me supplicaturum putat?

si est ut velit reducere uxorem, licet;

sin aliost animo, renumeret dotem huc, eat.

LA. ecce autem tu quoque proterve iracundus es!

PH. percontumax redisti huc nobis, Pamphile!

505   **LA.** decedet iam ira haec, etsi merito iratus est.

PH. quia paullum vobis accessit pecuniae,

sublati animi sunt. **LA.** etiam mecum litigas?

PH. deliberet renuntietque hodie mihi

velitne an non, ut alii, si huic non est, siet.

510   **LA.** Phidippe, ades, audi paucis - abiit. quid mea?

postremo inter se transigant ipsi ut lubet,

quando nec gnatus neque hic mi quicquam obtemperant,

have a tremendous yearning for her because I know from experience just how wonderful her feelings for me were. (490) I pray too that since fate is forcibly taking her from me, she may spend the rest of her life with a husband who's more fortunate than I.

PHIDIPPUS: It's in your power to prevent it.

LACHES: *(Forcefully)* If you had any sense - order her to come back.

PAMPHILUS: That's not my intention, father. (495) I shall pursue my mother's interests. *(Turns on his heels and leaves briskly)*

LACHES: Where are you off to? Don't go. I say, just a minute. Where are you going?

PHIDIPPUS: *(Angrily)* Such obstinacy!

LACHES: Well, Phidippus, didn't I tell you he'd take it badly? That's why I begged you to send your daughter back.

PHIDIPPUS: Really, I never thought he'd be so unfeeling! (500) Does he actually think I'll go down on my knees to him? If it turns out he wants to take his wife back, all well and good: if he has other ideas, he can give me back her dowry and go.

LACHES: There you are; you're becoming just the same: headstrong and angry.

PHIDIPPUS: *(Shouts after Pamphilus)* A nice stiff-necked attitude you've come back to us with, Pamphilus! (505)

LACHES: This anger of his will soon pass, even if he has good cause to feel indignant.

PHIDIPPUS: *(Rounds on Laches)* You people have become very high-minded just because you've come into a bit of money.

LACHES: Are you starting a quarrel with me as well?

PHIDIPPUS: He can think it over and let me know before tomorrow whether he wants her or not; she can be somebody else's wife, if she isn't his. *(Storms into his house)* (510)

LACHES: Phidippus, wait; just a word or two - he's gone. *(Shrugs his shoulders)* Oh well, what business is it of mine? When all is said and done, they can settle it between them how they like, since neither he nor my son pays any attention to me,

66

quae dico parvi pendunt. porto hoc iurgium
ad uxorem quoius haec fiunt consilio omnia,
515   atque in eam hoc omne quod mihi aegrest evomam.

(IV i) **Myrrina Phidippus**

MY. Perii, quid agam? quo me vortam? quid viro meo respondebo
misera? nam audivisse vocem pueri visust vagientis;
ita corripuit derepente tacitus sese ad filiam.
quod si rescierit peperisse eam, id qua causa clam me habuisse
520   dicam non edepol scio.
sed ostium concrepuit. credo ipsum exire ad me; nulla sum!
PH. uxor ubi me ad filiam ire sensit, se duxit foras;
atque eccam; video. quid ais, Myrrina? heus tibi dico. **MY**. mihine, vir?
PH. vir ego tuos sim? tu virum me aut hominem deputas adeo esse?
525   nam si utrumvis horum, mulier, umquam tibi visus forem,
non sic ludibrio tuis factis habitus essem. **MY**. quibus? **PH**. at rogitas?
peperit filia: hem, taces? ex qui? **MY**. istuc patrem rogare est aequom?
perii! ex quo censes nisi ex illo quoi datast nuptum obsecro?
PH. credo; neque adeo arbitrari patris est aliter. sed demiror
530   quid sit quam ob rem hunc tanto opere omnis nos celare volueris
partum, praesertim quom et recte et tempore suo pepererit.
adeon pervicaci esse animo ut puerum praeoptares perire,
ex quo firmiorem inter nos fore amicitiam posthac scires,
potius quam advorsum animi tui lubidinem esset cum illo nupta!
535   ego etiam illorum esse hanc culpam credidi, quae test penes.

or gives two hoots for what I say. I'll take this quarrel to my wife. It's her scheming that's the cause of all this; (515) so I'll vent all this vexation of mine on her.

(Disappears into his house. After a moment or two Phidippus' door opens and his wife rushes out in panic and despair)

(IV i)

MYRRINA: Disaster! What can I do? Which way can I turn? Whatever shall I tell my husband? Oh poor me! I'm sure he heard the child crying, the way he suddenly rushed into our daughter's room without saying a word. If he finds out she's had a baby, I really don't know what reason I can give him for having kept it a secret. (520) But there's the door. I do believe it's him coming out. I'm done for. *(She withdraws to a safe distance)*

PHIDIPPUS: When my wife realised I was going to our daughter's room, she came outside. *(Spots Myrrina)* There she is; I see her. Well Myrrina, what have you got to say? *(Shouts)* Hey, it's you I'm speaking to!

MYRRINA: *(Feigning innocence)* Me, husband?

PHIDIPPUS: *(Angrily)* Your husband am I? Do you regard me as your husband or even a human being? (525) If I'd ever been either of these in your eyes, woman, you wouldn't have made such a laughing stock of me in this way with your goings-on.

MYRRINA: What goings-on?

PHIDIPPUS: You ask that? Our daughter has had a baby. Well? Nothing to say? Who's the father?

MYRRINA: *(In a tone of astonishment)* Is that a proper question for her father to ask? Good grief! Who on earth do you think but the husband she was married to?

PHIDIPPUS: *(Shame-faced)* I suppose so. It hardly becomes a father to think otherwise. But I'm at a loss to know (530) the reason you were so anxious to hide this birth from us all, especially when it was a normal delivery and at the right time. Can it be you were so perverse that you preferred the death of the child, knowing it would strengthen the bond of friendship between our two families in the future, to her being married to a man who wasn't to your liking? (535) And *I* thought it was *their* fault, when in fact it's all *yours*.

MY. misera sum. **PH**. utinam sciam ita esse istuc! sed nunc mi in
mentem venit
de hac re quod locuta es olim, quom illum generum cepimus;
nam negabas nuptam posse filiam tuam te pati
cum eo qui meretricem amaret, qui pernoctaret foris.
540   **MY**. quamvis causam hunc suspicari quam ipsam veram mavolo.
PH. multo prius scivi quam tu illum habere amicam, Myrrina;
verum id vitium numquam decrevi esse ego adulescentiae;
nam id innatumst. at pol iam aderit se quoque etiam quom oderit.
sed ut olim te ostendisti, eadem esse nil cessavisti usque adhuc,
545   ut filiam ab eo abduceres neu quod ego egissem esset ratum.
id nunc res indicium haec facit quo pacto factum volueris.
MY. adeon me esse pervicacem censes, quoi mater siem,
ut eo essem animo, si ex usu esset nostro hoc matrimonium?
PH. tun prospicere aut iudicare nostram in rem quod sit potes?
550   audisti ex aliquo fortasse qui vidisse eum diceret
exeuntem aut intro euntem ad amicam. quid tum postea?
si modeste ac raro haec fecit, nonne ea dissimulare nos
magis humanumst quam dare operam id scire qui nos oderit?
nam si is posset ab ea sese derepente avellere
555   quicum tot consuesset annos, non eum hominem ducerem
nec virum satis firmum gnatae. **MY**. mitte adulescentem obsecro
et quae me peccasse ais. abi, solus solum conveni;
roga velitne uxorem an non. si est ut dicat velle se,
redde; sin est autem ut nolit, recte ego consului meae.
560   **PH**. siquidem ille ipse non volt et tu sensti in eo esse, Myrrina,
peccatum, aderam quoius consilio fuerat ea par prospici.
quam ob rem incendor ira esse ausam facere haec te iniussu meo.

MYRRINA: *(On the verge of tears)* I'm so unhappy.

PHIDIPPUS: *(Sarcastically)* I wish I knew it were so, but I've just remembered what you once said on the matter when we accepted him as our son-in-law: you said you couldn't stand to see your daughter married to someone who kept a mistress and spent his nights away from home. **(540)**

MYRRINA: *(Aside)* Better he suspect any reason than the real one.

PHIDIPPUS: I knew he had a mistress long before you did, Myrrina, but I never thought that a vice in a young man. It comes natural to them. The time will soon come, though, when he'll even hate himself for it. But to this day you haven't budged an inch from the position you held then - **(545)** of trying to get our daughter away from him and undoing the arrangements I made. This development today shows clearly what your intentions were.

MYRRINA: Do you really believe I could be so perverse as to take that attitude towards my own daughter if this marriage were to our advantage?

PHIDIPPUS: And have you the ability to foresee or judge just what *is* to our benefit? **(550)** Perhaps you heard someone saying he'd seen him going in and out of his mistress' house. *(Shrugs)* So what? If his visits were discreet and infrequent, isn't it more charitable for us to turn a blind eye to them rather than go out of our way to find out the facts and earn his hatred as a result? After all, if he were able to break off his relationship with her immediately, **(555)** after having gone with her for so many years, I'd not think him human or a stable enough match for our daughter.

MYRRINA: *(Forcefully)* Please, let's have no more of this young man or what you say are my misdeeds. Go and have a word with him in private and ask him whether he wants his wife or not. If it turns out he says he does, give her back; but if it turns out he doesn't, then I've done the right thing for my daughter. **(560)**

PHIDIPPUS: Well, even if he is unwilling and you realised the fault was on his side, Myrrina, I was there. It was only right that the matter be taken care of as I felt fit. That's why I'm incensed that you dared to take this course of action

interdico ne extulisse extra aedis puerum usquam velis.
sed ego stultior, meis dictis parere hanc qui postulem.
565 ibo intro atque edicam servis nequoquam ecferri sinant.
MY. nullam pol credo mulierem me miseriorem vivere.
nam ut hic laturus hoc sit, si ipsam rem ut siet resciverit,
non edepol clam me est, quom hoc quod leviust tam animo irato tulit;
nec qua via sententia eius possit mutari scio.
570 hoc mi unum ex plurumis miseriis relicuom fuerat malum,
si puerum ut tollam cogit, quoius nos qui sit nescimus pater.
nam quom compressast gnata, forma in tenebris nosci non quitast,
neque detractum ei tum quicquamst qui posset post nosci qui siet;
ipse eripuit vi, in digito quem habuit, virgini abiens anulum.
575 simul vereor Pamphilum ne orata nostra nequeat diutius
celare, quom sciet alienum puerum tolli pro suo.

(IV ii) Sostrata Pamphilus

SO. Non clam me est, gnate mi, tibi me esse suspectam uxorem tuam
propter meos mores hinc abisse, etsi ea dissimulas sedulo;
verum ita me di ament itaque optingant ex te quae exoptem mihi, ut
580 numquam sciens commerui merito ut caperet odium illam mei.
teque ante quod me amare rebar, ei rei firmasti fidem;
nam mi intus tuos pater narravit modo quo pacto me habueris
praepositam amori tuo. nunc tibi me certumst contra gratiam
referre ut apud me praemium esse positum pietati scias.
585 mi Pamphile, hoc et vobis et meae commodum famae arbitror:
ego rus abituram hinc cum tuo me esse certo decrevi patre,
ne mea praesentia obstet neu causa ulla restet relicua
quin tua Philumena ad te redeat.

without any permission from me. I forbid you to take the child anywhere outside the house. *(Aside)* But I'm the bigger fool in expecting her to pay any attention to what I say. **(565)** I'll go inside and give the servants strict instructions not to let it be taken anywhere outside. *(Goes inside, leaving his wife to pour out her troubles on her own)*

MYRRINA: Really, I don't think a more unhappy woman than myself draws breath! When he's reacted so angrily to something that's less serious like this, it's perfectly clear to me how he'll take it if he finds out the true state of affairs, and how he can be made to change his mind I've no idea. **(570)** After so many troubles it's the last straw if he forces me to keep the child when we don't know who its father is. At the time our daughter was raped she couldn't tell who it was in the dark, and didn't manage to seize anything from him by which his identity could be later established. *He* on the other hand pulled the girl's ring off her finger as he made his getaway. **(575)** I'm afraid too that when Pamphilus learns that another man's child is being brought up as his own, he won't feel able to keep secret any longer what we begged him to.

(Myrrina disappears inside. Out of Laches' house come Sostrata and Pamphilus. After a few moments Laches himself appears at the door and eavesdrops on their conversation)

(IV ii)

SOSTRATA: It hasn't escaped me, Pamphilus, even though you're careful to disguise the fact, that you've come to suspect it's because of my behaviour your wife has left our house. But heaven preserve me and may my expectations of you be granted - **(580)** I've never knowingly done anything wrong to justify her taking a dislike to me. As for my earlier belief in your affection towards me - well, you've now given me proof of it. Your father in fact has just told me inside how you've placed me before the object of your love. So now for my part I'm determined to return your kindness so that you know how much I appreciate your feelings of duty. **(585)** Pamphilus, my dear, this is what I think is best for the two of you and also for my reputation: I've made up my mind to go off to the country with your father so that my presence doesn't get in your way and so that there's no possible reason left for Philumena not returning to you.

PAM. quaeso quid istuc consilist?

illius stultitia victa ex urbe tu rus habitatum migres?

590   haud facies, neque sinam ut qui nobis, mater, male dictum velit,

mea pertinacia esse dicat factum, haud tua modestia.

tum tuas amicas te et cognatas deserere et festos dies

mea causa nolo. SO. nil pol iam istaec mihi res voluptatis ferunt.

dum aetatis tempus tulit, perfuncta satis sum; satias iam tenet

595   studiorum istorum. haec mihi nunc curast maxuma ut nequoi mea

longinquitas aetatis obstet mortemve exspectet meam.

hic video me esse invisam inmerito; tempust me concedere.

sic optume, ut ego opinor, omnis causas praecidam omnibus:

et me hac suspicione exsolvam et illis morem gessero.

600   sine me, obsecro, hoc effugere volgus quod male audit mulierum.

PAM. quam fortunatus ceteris sum rebus, absque una hac foret,

hanc matrem habens talem, illam autem uxorem! SO. obsecro, mi
      Pamphile,

non tute incommodam rem, ut quaeque est, in animum induces pati?

si cetera ita sunt ut vis itaque uti esse ego illa existumo,

605   mi gnate, da veniam hanc mihi, redduc illam. PAM. vae misero mihi!

SO. et mihi quidem; nam haec res non minus me male habet quam te,
      gnate mi.

(IV iii) Laches Sostrata Pamphilus

LA. Quem cum istoc sermonem habueris, procul hinc stans accepi, uxor.

istuc est sapere, qui ubiquomque opus sit animum possis flectere,

quod sit faciundum fortasse post, idem hoc nunc si feceris.

610   SO. fors fuat pol. LA. abi rus ergo hinc; ibi ego te et tu me feres.

PAMPHILUS: *(Appalled)* For goodness sake, what kind of idea is that? Give in to her stupidity and leave the city to live in the country! **(590)** You'll do no such thing, and I'll not have anyone who wants us ill-spoken of, mother, saying it was the result of my obstinacy and not your good nature. What's more, I don't want you giving up your friends and relations and the public festivals for my sake.

SOSTRATA: But things like that don't give me any pleasure now. While my younger days allowed, I enjoyed them well enough; now I've had enough **(595)** of such pursuits. My chief concern at the moment is for my advancing years not to be a burden to anybody or for people to look forward to my death. Here in town I see I'm disliked, though through no fault of my own; so it's time for me to go. This is the best way, I think, of removing all the reasons for discontent from everybody - I'll clear myself of suspicion and fall in with their wishes. **(600)** Please, I beg you, allow me to escape this common reproach of womankind.

PAMPHILUS: How fortunate I am in other respects - or would be but for this one thing - with a mother like you and a wife like her!

SOSTRATA: Please, Pamphilus dear, can't you bring yourself to put up with one inconvenience, whatever it is? If everything else is as you want it and as I take it to be, **(605)** son, do me this one favour and take her back.

PAMPHILUS: Oh, I'm devastated!

SOSTRATA: Me too. This affair distresses me no less than you, son.

(IV iii)

LACHES: *(Comes forward)* I've been standing some distance away listening to the conversation you've been having with Pamphilus, my dear. It shows sound sense if you're able to bend before the wind when necessary and do today what you might perhaps be forced to do later. **(610)**

SOSTRATA: Amen to that.

LACHES: So off you go to the country, and once there I'll put up with you, and you with me.

SO. spero ecastor. LA. i ergo intro et compone quae tecum simul
ferantur. dixi. SO. ita ut iubes faciam. PAM. pater!
LA. quid vis, Pamphile? PAM. hinc abire matrem? minime. LA. quid
    ita istuc vis?
PAM. quia de uxore incertus sum etiam quid sim facturus. LA. quid est?
615   quid vis facere nisi reducere? PAM. equidem cupio et vix contineor,
sed non minuam meum consilium. ex usu quod est id persequar.
credo ea gratia concordes, si non reducam, fore.
LA. nescias; verum id tua refert nil utrum illaec fecerint
quando haec aberit. odiosa haec est aetas adulescentulis;
620   e medio aequom excedere est; postremo nos iam fabulae
sumus, Pamphile, "senex atque anus".
sed video Phidippum egredi per tempus; accedamus.

(IV iv) **Phidippus Laches Pamphilus**

PH. Tibi quoque edepol sum iratus, Philumena,
graviter quidem; nam hercle factumst abs te turpiter;
625   etsi tibi causast de hac re: mater te inpulit.
huic vero nullast. LA. opportune te mihi,
Phidippe, in ipso tempore ostendis. PH. quid est?
PAM. quid respondebo his? aut quo pacto hoc aperiam?
LA. dic filiae rus concessuram hinc Sostratam,
630   ne revereatur minus iam quo redeat domum. PH. ah
nullam de his rebus culpam commeruit tua;
a Myrrina haec sunt mea uxore exorta omnia.

SOSTRATA: That's very much my hope.

LACHES: Inside with you then, and get together the things to go with you. That's all I have to say.

SOSTRATA: I'll do as you order. *(She goes inside)*

PAMPHILUS: Father.

LACHES: What is it, Pamphilus?

PAMPHILUS: Mother leave town? Impossible!

LACHES: Why don't you want her to?

PAMPHILUS: Because I'm still undecided what to do about my wife.

LACHES: *(Astonished)* What's that? **(615)** What do you intend to do if not to take her back?

PAMPHILUS: *(Aside)* That's really what I want to do and I can hardly hold myself back, but I'll not weaken my resolve. I'll press on with what's best. *(Aloud)* I think they'll be reconciled to one another, actually, if I don't take her back.

LACHES: You can't tell. But really, it's of no relevance to you which course of action they take once your mother here is out of the way. People of our age are a pain to young folk. **(620)** It's best if we slip away. In short Pamphilus, we're now like the story, "The Old Couple". *(Phidippus' door opens and the old man appears, still talking to those inside)* But there's Phidippus coming out just at the right moment. Let's go to him.

(IV iv)

PHIDIPPUS: I'm angry with you too, Philumena, I really am - very angry indeed. You've behaved extremely badly, **(625)** though you've some excuse for doing so - your mother put you up to it. She certainly has no excuse. *(Turns and sees Laches)*

LACHES: Ah, Phidippus, you've appeared just at the right moment.

PHIDIPPUS: Why's that?

PAMPHILUS: *(Aside)* What shall I tell them? How shall I explain it?

LACHES: Tell your daughter that Sostrata is going to retire to the country, **(630)** so now she needn't be afraid to return home.

PHIDIPPUS: But your wife's done nothing to deserve any blame in this affair. It's my wife Myrrina who's created this whole situation.

76

PAM. mutatio fit. PH. ea nos perturbat, Lache.
PAM. dum ne redducam, turbent porro quam velint.
635 PH. ego, Pamphile, esse inter nos, si fieri potest,
adfinitatem hanc sane perpetuam volo;
sin est ut aliter tua siet sententia,
accipias puerum. PAM. sensit peperisse; occidi!
LA. puerum? quem puerum? PH. natus est nobis nepos;
640 nam abducta a vobis praegnas fuerat filia,
neque fuisse praegnatem umquam ante hunc scivi diem.
LA. bene, ita me di ament, nuntias, et gaudeo
natum illum et tibi illam salvam. sed quid mulieris
uxorem habes aut quibus moratam moribus?
645 nosne hoc celatos tam diu! nequeo satis
quam hoc mihi videtur factum prave proloqui.
PH. non tibi illud factum minus placet quam mihi, Lache.
PAM. etiamsi dudum fuerat ambiguom hoc mihi,
nunc non est quom eam sequitur alienus puer.
650 LA. nulla tibi, Pamphile, hic iam consultatiost.
PAM. perii! LA. hunc videre saepe optabamus diem
quom ex te esset aliquis qui te appellaret patrem.
evenit: habeo gratiam dis. PAM. nullu' sum!
LA. redduc uxorem ac noli advorsari mihi.
655 PAM. pater, si ex me illa liberos vellet sibi
aut sese mecum nuptam, satis certo scio,
non clam me haberet quae celasse intellego.
nunc quom eius alienum esse animum a me sentiam -
nec conventurum inter nos posthac arbitror -
660 quam ob rem redducam? LA. mater quod suasit sua
adulescens mulier fecit. mirandumne id est?
censen te posse reperire ullam mulierem
quae careat culpa? an quia non delincunt viri?

PAMPHILUS: *(Aside)* That's quite an about-turn!

PHIDIPPUS: She's the one who's causing us problems, Laches.

PAMPHILUS: *(Aside)* So long as I don't have to take her back, they can go on having as many problems as they like. **(635)**

PHIDIPPUS: *(Turns to Pamphilus)* My own wish, Pamphilus, is that this marriage-tie between us should, if at all possible, remain unbroken. If, however, it turns out you have other ideas, at least take the child.

PAMPHILUS: *(Aside)* Damn! He's found out about the birth.

LACHES: *(Suddenly pricking up his ears)* Child? What child?

PHIDIPPUS: We've got ourselves a grandson. **(640)** My daughter was expecting when she was moved from your house, though I had no idea she was until today.

LACHES: Well bless me, that's wonderful news you're bringing. I'm delighted the child's been born and that Philumena is safe and well. *(Lowers his voice)* But what kind of a woman do you have for a wife, and what kind of behaviour is this? **(645)** To think that we've been kept in the dark about it for so long! I can't begin to describe how improper it strikes me as being.

PHIDIPPUS: I don't like it one bit more than you do, Laches.

PAMPHILUS: *(Aside)* If I had any doubts about it before, I've none now, seeing that another man's child is coming with her. **(650)**

LACHES: Under the circumstances you've no room for debate now, Pamphilus.

PAMPHILUS: *(Aside)* Help!

LACHES: This is the day we've often longed to see - when you would have a son to call you father. Well, here it is, and thank God for it.

PAMPHILUS: *(Aside)* I'm finished!

LACHES: Take your wife back and let's have no more argument. **(655)**

PAMPHILUS: Father, if she wanted to have children by me or to be my wife, she wouldn't have kept secret from me what I see she *has* concealed. I'm pretty sure of it. I can see now that her feelings have turned against me - and I don't think there can be harmony between us in the future - **(660)** so why should I take her back?

LACHES: The girl's young and did what her mother told her to. Is that at all surprising? Do you think you can find any woman who's perfect, or is it that men have no faults?

PH. vosmet videte iam, Lache et tu Pamphile,
665   remissan opus sit vobis redductan domum.
667   neutra in re vobis difficultas a me erit -
666   uxor quid faciat in manu non est mea.
        sed quid faciemus puero? **LA**. ridicule rogas.
        quidquid futurumst, huic suom reddas scilicet
670   ut alamus nostrum. **PAM**. quem ipse neglexit pater,
        ego alam? **LA**. quid dixti? eho an non alemus, Pamphile?
        prodemus quaeso potius? quae haec amentiast?
        enimvero prorsus iam tacere non queo;
        nam cogis ea quae nolo ut praesente hoc loquar.
675   ignarum censes tuarum lacrumarum esse me
        aut quid sit id quod sollicitare ad hunc modum?
        primum hanc ubi dixti causam, te propter tuam
        matrem non posse habere hanc uxorem domi,
        pollicitast ea se concessuram ex aedibus.
680   nunc postquam ademptam hanc quoque tibi causam vides,
        puer quia clam test natus, nactus alteram es.
        erras tui animi si me esse ignarum putas.
        aliquando tandem huc animum ut adiungas tuom,
        quam longum spatium amandi amicam tibi dedi!
685   sumptus quos fecisti in eam quam animo aequo tuli!
        egi atque oravi tecum uxorem ut duceres;
        tempus dixi esse; inpulsu duxisti meo.
        quae tum obsecutus mihi fecisti ut decuerat.
        nunc animum rursum ad meretricem induxti tuom,
690   quoi tu obsecutus facis huic adeo iniuriam;
        nam in eandem vitam te revolutum denuo
        video esse. **PAM**. mene? **LA**. te ipsum, et facis iniuriam;
        confingis falsas causas ad discordiam
        ut cum illa vivas, testem hanc quom abs te amoveris.

PHIDIPPUS: *(Exasperated)* You two sort it out between you, Laches - you too, Pamphilus - **(665)** whether you want her sent back or kept at home, that is. Either way you'll have no trouble from me; what my wife does, though, is out of my hands. But what shall we do about the child?

LACHES: That's a daft question. Whatever happens, you must of course give Pamphilus here his child **(670)** so we can bring it up - he is ours after all.

PAMPHILUS: *(Aside)* When its own father hasn't taken any interest in it, should I bring it up?

LACHES: *(Hearing Pamphilus' final words)* What did you say? What, not bring it up, Pamphilus? Are we then to abandon it instead? What madness is this? Goodness gracious, I really can't hold my tongue any longer! You're forcing me to say things I don't want to in front of Phidippus here. **(675)** Do you think I haven't noticed those tears of yours and don't know why it is you're all upset like this? At first you claimed the reason you couldn't have Philumena at home as your wife was because of your mother; so your mother promised to quit the house. **(680)** Now you see that you've been deprived of this excuse, you've found yourself another in the fact that the child was born without your knowledge. If you think I don't know what's going on in your mind, you're mistaken. After all the time I let you carry on your affair with a mistress so that eventually you might bring your mind round to matrimony! **(685)** After all my patience in putting up with the bills you ran up because of her! I begged and pleaded with you to take a wife; I told you it was time you did, and in response to my prompting you *did* get married. By complying with my wishes then you did what was proper. Now, you've given your heart back to your mistress **(690)** and, what's more, your behaviour in complying with her wishes is an affront to your wife here. It's clear to me in fact you've gone back to your old way of life again.

PAMPHILUS: Me?

LACHES: Yes you; and what you're doing is an affront - you're trumping up false excuses for a breakdown of relations so you can live with that woman once you've

695   sensitque adeo uxor; nam ei causa alia quae fuit

quam ob rem abs te abiret? **PH.** plane hic divinat; nam id est.

PAM. dabo iusiurandum nil esse istorum mihi. **LA.** ah,

redduc uxorem aut quam ob rem non opus sit cedo.

PAM. non est nunc tempus. **LA.** puerum accipias; nam is quidem

700   in culpa non est; post de matre videro.

PAM. omnibus modis miser sum nec quid agam scio.

tot nunc me rebus miserum concludit pater.

abibo hinc, praesens quando promoveo parum;

nam puerum iniussu credo non tollent meo,

705   praesertim in ea re quom sit mi adiutrix socrus.

LA. fugis? hem, nec quicquam certi respondes mihi?

num tibi videtur esse apud sese? sine.

puerum, Phidippe, mihi cedo; ego alam. **PH.** maxume.

non mirum fecit uxor si hoc aegre tulit.

710   amarae mulieres sunt, non facile haec ferunt.

propterea haec irast; nam ipsa narravit mihi.

id ego hoc praesente tibi nolueram dicere,

neque illi credebam primo; nunc verum palamst;

nam omnino abhorrere animum huic video a nuptiis.

715   **LA.** quid ergo agam, Phidippe? quid das consili?

PH. quid agas? meretricem hanc primum adeundam censeo.

oremus, accusemus, gravius denique

minitemur si cum illo habuerit rem postea...

LA. faciam ut mones. eho puere, curre ad Bacchidem hanc

720   vicinam nostram; huc evoca verbis meis.

et te oro porro in hac re adiutor sis mihi.

got rid of Philumena as a witness. **(695)** What's more, your wife realised this. What other reason could she have for leaving you?

PHIDIPPUS: *(Aside)* Laches must have second sight. That's it exactly.

PAMPHILUS: None of these charges against me is true, I swear.

LACHES: Then take your wife back, or tell us why you can't.

PAMPHILUS: *(Weakly)* Now's not the time.

LACHES: Then take the child. *It* certainly **(700)** isn't to blame and I'll see about its mother later.

PAMPHILUS: *(Aside as he turns away)* I'm completely and utterly devastated! I just don't know what to do. My father's driving me into a corner with all these arguments, damn it! I'll make a getaway since I'm not doing much good by staying around. They won't acknowledge the child against my wishes, I don't think, **(705)** especially since I have my mother-in-law on my side in this. *(Rushes off)*

LACHES: Running away? Hey! Aren't you going to give me a proper answer? *(Turns to Phidippus)* Do you think he's in his right mind? Well, let him go. Give me the child, Phidippus. I'll bring it up.

PHIDIPPUS: Very well. No wonder my wife was annoyed at the situation. **(710)** Women are a disagreeable lot and don't easily stand for this kind of thing. That's what her resentment is all about. She told me so herself. I didn't like to tell you with Pamphilus here, and at first I didn't believe her, but now the truth is clear. I can see that temperamentally he's totally set against married life. **(715)**

LACHES: So what should I do, Phidippus? What advice can you give?

PHIDIPPUS: What should you do? First of all I think we should make an approach to this mistress of his, reproach her, and finally, issue a stiff threat that if she has anything to do with him in future...

LACHES: I'll do as you advise. *(Calls towards his house)* Boy! Run over **(720)** to our neighbour Bacchis there and call her out here to me. *(A young slave appears and runs to Bacchis' house. Laches turns to Phidippus)* And please, back me up in this.

PH. ah,
iamdudum dixi idemque nunc dico, Lache:
manere adfinitatem hanc inter nos volo,
si ullo modo est ut possit, quod spero fore.
725   sed vin adesse me una dum istam convenis?
LA. immo vero abi, aliquam puero nutricem para.

(V i) **Bacchis Laches**

BA. Non hoc de nihilost quod Laches me nunc conventam esse expetit,
nec pol me multum fallit quin quod suspicor sit quod velit.
LA. videndumst ne minus propter iram hanc impetrem quam possiem,
730   aut nequid faciam plus quod post me minus fecisse satiu' sit.
adgrediar. Bacchis, salve.
BA. salve, Lache. LA. credo edepol te non nil mirari, Bacchis,
quid sit quapropter te huc foras puerum evocare iussi.
BA. ego pol quoque etiam timida sum quom venit mi in mentem quae
        sim,
735   ne nomen mihi quaesti obsiet; nam mores facile tutor.
LA. si vera dicis, nil tibist a me pericli, mulier;
nam iam aetate ea sum ut non siet peccato mi ignosci aequom;
quo magis omnis res cautius ne temere faciam adcuro.
nam si id facis facturave es bonas quod par est facere,
740   inscitum offerre iniuriam tibi inmerenti iniquom est.
BA. est magna ecastor gratia de istac re quam tibi habeam;
nam qui post factam iniuriam se expurget parum mi prosit.
sed quid istuc est? LA. meum receptas filium ad te Pamphilum. BA. ah.
LA. sine dicam. uxorem hanc prius quam duxit, vostrum amorem pertuli.
745   mane: nondum etiam dixi id quod volui. hic nunc uxorem habet:
quaere alium tibi firmiorem dum tibi tempus consulendi est;
nam neque ille hoc animo erit aetatem neque pol tu eadem istac aetate.

PHIDIPPUS: Well, as I said before, I say again now, Laches - I want this marriage alliance between us to continue, if that's at all possible, and I hope it will be. **(725)** But do you want me around while you deal with the woman?

LACHES: Well, no. You go and find a nurse for the child. *(Phidippus leaves. Bacchis emerges from her house accompanied by two maids and Laches' slave, who returns home)*

(V i)

BACCHIS: *(Aside)* It's not for nothing Laches wants me to get in touch with him, and unless I'm very much mistaken, I've a pretty good idea what it is he wants.

LACHES: *(Aside)* I have to be careful that in my present angry state I don't achieve less than I otherwise could, **(730)** or that I don't overdo things and later regret it. I'll approach her. *(With formal politeness)* Good day, Bacchis.

BACCHIS: Good day, Laches.

LACHES: I expect you must be wondering, Bacchis, why it is I told the boy to call you out here.

BACCHIS: Yes and, considering what I am, apprehensive too **(735)** that the reputation of my profession might cause prejudice against me - my actual conduct I can easily defend.

LACHES: If what you're saying is true, madam, you're in no danger from me. I'm now of an age when I can't expect forgiveness if I step out of line. For that reason I take all the more care to avoid indiscretions. If you behave now or in the future as befits an honest woman, **(740)** it would be wrong of me to insult you in some heavy-handed manner when you don't deserve it.

BACCHIS: *(Tartly)* For that at least I have cause to be much obliged to you: an apology after the wrong is done isn't much use to me. But what's this all about?

LACHES: You're receiving visits from my son Pamphilus.

BACCHIS: But...

LACHES: Let me speak. Before he married I put up with the love-affair between you two. *(Bacchis moves to intervene)* **(745)** No, hold on; I haven't told you yet what I wanted. Now he is married, so while you still have time for reflection, look for someone else who'll be more devoted to you. Pamphilus won't have these same feelings all his life and you won't always be as young as you now are.

BA. quis id ait? **LA.** socrus. **BA.** men? **LA.** te ipsam; et filiam abduxit suam,

puerumque ob eam rem clam voluit, natus qui est, exstinguere.

750 **BA.** aliud si scirem qui firmare meam apud vos possem fidem

sanctius quam iusiurandum, id pollicerer tibi, Lache,

me segregatum habuisse, uxorem ut duxit, a me Pamphilum.

LA. lepida es; sed scin quid volo potius sodes facias? **BA.** quid vis? cedo.

LA. eas ad mulieres huc intro atque istuc iusiurandum idem

755 polliceare illis. exple animum is teque hoc crimine expedi.

BA. faciam quod pol, si esset alia ex hoc quaestu, haud faceret, scio,

ut de tali causa nuptae mulieri se ostenderet.

sed nolo esse falsa fama gnatum suspectum tuom,

nec leviorem vobis, quibus est minime aequom, eum viderier

760 inmerito; nam meritus de me est quod queam illi ut commodem.

LA. facilem benivolumque lingua tua iam tibi me reddidit.

nam non sunt solae arbitratae haec; ego quoque etiam credidi.

nunc quam ego te esse praeter nostram opinionem comperi,

fac eadem ut sis porro; nostra utere amicitia ut voles.

765 aliter si facies - reprimam me ne aegre quicquam ex me audias.

verum hoc moneo unum: qualis sim amicus aut quid possiem

potius quam inimicus, periclum facias.

(V ii) **Phidippus Laches Bacchis**

PH. Nil apud me tibi

defieri patiar quin quod opus sit benigne praebeatur;

sed quom tu satura atque ebria eris, puer ut satur sit facito.

BACCHIS: Who's making this claim?

LACHES: His mother-in-law.

BACCHIS: About me?

LACHES: Yes you, and she's taken her daughter back, and as a result she planned to do away in secret with the child that's been born. **(750)**

BACCHIS: If I knew of any other means by which I could strengthen your belief in what I say, Laches, any means more sacred than an oath, I'd give you it as an assurance that I have kept Pamphilus away from me ever since he got married.

LACHES: That's very good of you, but do you know what I'd rather you did - if you're agreeable?

BACCHIS: What is it? Tell me.

LACHES: Go inside to the women here and give *them* this same assurance. **(755)** Set *their* minds at rest and clear yourself of this charge.

BACCHIS: Very well. I'll do what anyone else in my profession certainly wouldn't; of that I'm sure: appear before a married woman for such a reason, that is. But I don't want your son to be under suspicion because of some false rumour, or for you to think him irresponsible when he doesn't deserve it - you're the last people who should do that. **(760)** For my part he deserves all the help I can give him.

LACHES: What you say has restored you to my favour and goodwill. The women weren't alone in their opinion; it was mine too. Now that I've found you're quite different from what we imagined, make sure you remain so in the future and you'll enjoy our friendship as you wish. **(765)** Should you behave otherwise - but no, I'll keep quiet in case you hear anything from me that may upset you. But I give you this one piece of advice: find out what sort of a friend I am and what I'm capable of as such rather than what sort of enemy. *(Phidippus returns along the street with a nurse)*

(V ii)

PHIDIPPUS: *(To the nurse)* I'll see that you want for nothing in my house and that you have plenty of anything you need. But when you've had enough to eat and drink, make sure that the child is satisfied too.

(The nurse disappears into Phidippus' house)

770   **LA.** noster socer, video, venit; puero nutricem adducit.

Phidippe, Bacchis deierat persancte... **PH.** haecin east? **LA.** haec est.

PH. nec pol istae metuont deos neque eas respicere deos opinor.

BA. ancillas dedo; quolubet cruciatu per me exquire.

haec res hic agitur: Pamphilo me facere ut redeat uxor

775   oportet; quod si perficio, non paenitet me famae

solam fecisse id quod aliae meretrices facere fugitant.

LA. Phidippe, nostras mulieres suspectas fuisse falso

nobis in re ipsa invenimus; porro hanc nunc experiamur.

nam si compererit crimini tua se uxor credidisse,

780   missam iram faciet; sin autem est ob eam rem iratus gnatus

quod peperit uxor clam, id levest; cito ab eo haec ira abscedet.

profecto in hac re nil malist quod sit discidio dignum.

PH. velim quidem hercle. **LA.** exquire; adest; quod satis sit faciet ipsa.

PH. quid mihi istaec narras? an quia non tute ipse dudum audisti

785   de hac re animus meus ut sit, Laches? illis modo explete animum.

LA. quaeso edepol, Bacchis, quod mihi es pollicita tute ut serves.

BA. ob eam rem vin ego intro eam? **LA.** i, atque exple animum is, coge

ut credant.

BA. eo, etsi scio pol is fore meum conspectum invisum hodie;

nam nupta meretrici hostis est, a viro ubi segregatast.

LACHES: *(770)* There's our father-in-law coming; he's bringing a nurse for the child. *(Aloud to attract attention)* Phidippus, Bacchis here swears solemnly...

PHIDIPPUS: *(Turns and looks Bacchis up and down)* Is *this* her?

LACHES: Yes it is.

PHIDIPPUS: Well *her* sort don't stand in fear of the gods, and I don't suppose the gods give a second thought to them.

BACCHIS: Here are my maidservants; you have my permission to examine them using whatever method of torture you like. The point at issue is this: I have to make Pamphilus' wife go back to him. *(775)* If I succeed in this I shall have no regrets when it's said of me that I alone did what other women in my profession try to avoid.

LACHES: *(Attempting an air of assurance)* Phidippus, we've discovered in the event that we wrongly suspected our wives, so let's now put Bacchis here to the test. If your wife finds that she gave credence to what was a groundless charge, *(780)* she'll let her resentment drop. And if my son is annoyed simply because his wife gave birth without revealing the fact, why, that's a mere trifle - he'll soon get over his resentment. Certainly there's nothing in this affair serious enough to justify divorce.

PHIDIPPUS: That's certainly my hope.

LACHES: *(Indicates Bacchis)* Question away; here she is; she'll do whatever's necessary.

PHIDIPPUS: Why tell me all this? Didn't you yourself hear *(785)* what my feelings are on this a while back, Laches? It's only *their* minds you two should set at rest. *(Goes indoors)*

LACHES: Bacchis, in heaven's name, I beg you to keep the promise you made me.

BACCHIS: *(Nervously)* You really want me to go inside about this matter?

LACHES: Yes, go and set their minds at rest. Make them believe you.

BACCHIS: Then I'll go, though I'm well aware they'll absolutely hate the sight of me. Once a wife is put aside by her husband, she becomes his mistress' sworn enemy.

790   **LA.** at haec amicae erunt, ubi quam ob rem adveneris resciscent.

    [**PH.** at easdem amicas fore tibi promitto, rem ubi cognorint;]

    nam illas errore et te simul suspicione exsolves.

    BA. perii, pudet Philumenae. me sequimini huc intro ambae.

    LA. quid est quod mihi malim quam quod huic intellego evenire,

795   ut gratiam ineat sine suo dispendio et mihi prosit?

    nam si est ut haec nunc Pamphilum vere ab se segregarit,

    scit sibi nobilitatem ex eo et rem natam et gloriam esse:

    referet gratiam ei unaque nos sibi opera amicos iunget.

(V iii) **Parmeno Bacchis**

    PAR. Edepol ne meam erus esse operam deputat parvi preti,

800   qui ob rem nullam misit frustra ubi totum desedi diem,

    Myconium hospitem dum exspecto in arce Callidemidem.

    itaque ineptus hodie dum illi sedeo, ut quisque venerat,

    accedebam: "adulescens, dicdum quaeso mi, es tu Myconius?"

    "non sum." "at Callidemides?" "non." "hospitem ecquem Pamphilum

805   hic habes?" omnes negabant; neque eum quemquam esse arbitror.

    denique hercle iam pudebat; abii. sed quid Bacchidem

    ab nostro adfine exeuntem video? quid huic hic est rei?

    BA. Parmeno, opportune te offers. propere curre ad Pamphilum.

    PAR. quid eo? **BA.** dic me orare ut veniat. **PAR.** ad te? **BA.** immo ad

       Philumenam.

810   **PAR.** quid rei est? **BA.** tua quod nil refert percontari desinas.

LACHES: (790) But they'll be your friends when they find out why you've come; for at one and the same time you'll be freeing them from their misapprehensions and yourself from suspicion.

BACCHIS: Oh dear, I'm overcome with embarrassment before Philumena. You two maids follow me inside here. *(She moves hesitantly towards Phidippus' door and enters)*

LACHES: There's nothing I'd rather happen to me than what I see happening to Bacchis: (795) making herself popular at no cost to herself and doing me a favour as well. If it's the case that she really *has* now broken off with Pamphilus, she knows she'll win honour, fortune, and renown from it: she'll be demonstrating her gratitude to him and at the same time link us to her in friendship.

(Goes inside his own house. From the right Parmeno trudges into view, evidently exhausted and fed-up)

(V iii)

PARMENO: My God, master doesn't put much value on my hard work, that's for sure, (800) sending me off on a wild-goose chase to sit about all day for nothing, waiting on the Citadel for Callidemides, the man he stayed with on Myconos. There I sat like a complete idiot and every time anyone came along I approached him with: "Please sir, tell me: are you from Myconos?" "No, I'm not." "Then is your name Callidemides?" "No." "Have you a friend here called Pamphilus?" (805) They all said no. In fact I don't think such a person exists. In the end I began to get thoroughly fed-up and left. *(Phidippus' door opens and Bacchis appears)* But why do I see Bacchis coming out of our in-laws'? What business has *she* got there?

BACCHIS: *(Sees Parmeno)* Parmeno, you've appeared just in time. Quick, run and find Pamphilus.

PARMENO: *(Peeved)* What for?

BACCHIS: Tell him I'm asking him to come.

PARMENO: To you?

BACCHIS: No, to Philumena. (810)

PARMENO: What's this all about?

BACCHIS: Don't ask questions when it's none of your business.

PAR. nil aliud dicam? **BA.** etiam: cognosse anulum illum Myrrinam
gnatae suae fuisse quem ipsus olim mi dederat. **PAR.** scio.
tantumne est? **BA.** tantum; aderit continuo hoc ubi ex te audiverit.
sed cessas? **PAR.** minime equidem; nam hodie mihi potestas haud datast:
815   ita cursando atque ambulando totum hunc contrivi diem.
    BA. quantam obtuli adventu meo laetitiam Pamphilo hodie!
quot commodas res attuli! quot autem ademi curas!
gnatum ei restituo, qui paene harunc ipsiusque opera periit;
uxorem, quam numquam est ratus posthac se habiturum, reddo;
820   qua re suspectus suo patri et Phidippo fuit, exsolvi.
hic adeo his rebus anulus fuit initium inveniundis.
nam memini abhinc mensis decem fere ad me nocte prima
confugere anhelantem domum sine comite, vini plenum,
cum hoc anulo. extimui ilico: "mi Pamphile," inquam "amabo,
825   quid exanimatu's obsecro? aut unde anulum istum nactu's?
dic mi." ille alias res agere se simulare. postquam id video,
nescioquid suspicarier mage coepi, instare ut dicat.
homo se fatetur vi in via nescioquam compressisse,
dicitque sese illi anulum, dum luctat, detraxisse.
830   eum haec cognovit Myrrina in digito modo me habente;
rogat unde sit; narro omnia haec; inde est cognitio facta
Philumenam compressam esse ab eo et filium inde hunc natum.
haec tot propter me gaudia illi contigisse laetor,
etsi hoc meretrices aliae nolunt; neque enim est in rem nostram
835   ut quisquam amator nuptiis laetetur. verum ecastor
numquam animum quaesti gratia ad malas adducam partis.
ego dum illo licitumst usa sum benigno et lepido et comi.
incommode mihi nuptiis evenit, factum fateor;
at pol me fecisse arbitror ne id merito mi eveniret.
840   multa ex quo fuerint commoda, eius incommoda aequomst ferre.

PARMENO: There's nothing else I'm to tell him?

BACCHIS: Yes: Myrrina has recognised that ring he gave me some time back as having belonged to her daughter.

PARMENO: I understand. Is that all?

BACCHIS: That's all. He'll be here like a flash when he hears this from you. *(Parmeno shows no signs of moving)* But what are you hanging around for?

PARMENO: *(Sarcastically)* That's the last thing I'm doing: haven't been given the chance to all day. **(815)** I've spent the whole of today on the go and running about. *(Parmeno drags himself off. Bacchis turns to the audience)*

BACCHIS: What happiness I've given Pamphilus today by coming here! How many blessings I've brought! How many worries I've removed! I'm giving him back a child that almost perished - thanks to himself and the women here - restoring a wife to him he never expected to live with again; **(820)** I've freed him from his father's and Phidippus' suspicions, and it was this very ring that sparked off all these discoveries. I remember how about ten months ago he came rushing in to me just after dark, all out of breath, no one with him, the worse for drink, and carrying this ring. Straight away I was filled with alarm: "Goodness, Pamphilus dear", I said, **(825)** "why on earth are you in this agitated state, and where did you get that ring from? Come along, tell me." He pretended he hadn't heard me. When I saw this, I began to get even more suspicious and pressed him to come clean. The fellow admitted he'd raped some girl in the street and said he'd pulled the ring off her finger in the struggle. **(830)** It's this ring that Myrrina here recognised me wearing on my finger just now. She asked where it came from; I told her everything and from that came the realisation it was Philumena who'd been raped by him and that the child here is his son. I'm glad to have been the cause of all this happiness for him, though it isn't what other women of my sort aim at - it's not in our interest **(835)** that any lover should be happily married. But really, I'll never bring myself to be nasty for the sake of profit. While circumstances permitted I found him kind, courteous, and loving. His marriage was a bit of bad luck for me, I admit, but I think my conduct has been such that when it came, it didn't serve me right. **(840)** When you've had a lot of good times from a man, it's only fair to put up with the bad times he causes.

(V iv) **Pamphilus Parmeno Bacchis**

PAM. Vide, mi Parmeno, etiam sodes, ut mi haec certa et clara attuleris,
ne me in breve conicias tempus gaudio hoc falso frui.
PAR. visumst. **PAM.** certen? **PAR.** certe. **PAM.** deus sum si hoc itast.
    PAR. verum reperies.
PAM. manedum sodes; timeo ne aliud credam atque aliud nunties.
845   **PAR.** maneo. **PAM.** sic te dixe opinor, invenisse Myrrinam
Bacchidem anulum suom habere. **PAR.** factum. **PAM.** eum quem olim
    ei dedi;
eaque hoc te mihi nuntiare iussit. itanest factum? **PAR.** ita, inquam.
PAM. quis me est fortunatior venustatisque adeo plenior?
egon pro hoc te nuntio qui donem? qui? qui? nescio.
850   **PAR.** at ego scio. **PAM.** quid? **PAR.** nihilo enim;
nam neque in nuntio neque in me ipso tibi boni quid sit scio.
PAM. egon qui ab Orco mortuom me reducem in lucem feceris
sinam sine munere a me abire? ah nimium me ignavom putas.

(From one of the side entrances Pamphilus appears with Parmeno in a state of high excitement)

(V iv)

PAMPHILUS: Do please make certain once again, Parmeno, that this information you've brought me is absolutely correct, and that you're not enticing me into some temporary state of misplaced happiness.

PARMENO: I am certain.

PAMPHILUS: Absolutely?

PARMENO: Absolutely.

PAMPHILUS: If that's the case, I'm in heaven.

PARMENO: You'll find it's true.

PAMPHILUS: *(Halts suddenly)* Wait a minute, though, I'm afraid you may be saying one thing and I believing another. **(845)**

PARMENO: I'm waiting.

PAMPHILUS: What I understand you to say is this: Myrrina has discovered Bacchis has her ring.

PARMENO: That's it.

PAMPHILUS: The one I gave her some time ago, and she told you to tell me this. Is that it?

PARMENO: That's it. That's what I'm saying.

PAMPHILUS: *(Overjoyed again)* Who is there more fortunate or, for that matter, luckier in love than I? What reward can I give you for this piece of news? What, what indeed? I just don't know. **(850)**

PARMENO: I do.

PAMPHILUS: What then?

PARMENO: *(Throws up his hands)* Nothing of course, since I can't see what benefit you've had from either the news or myself.

PAMPHILUS: What? Can I let you go without a reward when you've brought me back from Hell, back into the light of day, dead as I was? *(Puts his arm round the slave's shoulder)* Ah, you must think me singularly churlish. *(Catches sight of*

sed Bacchidem eccam video stare ante ostium;
855   me exspectat credo; adibo. **BA**. salve, Pamphile.
    PAM. o Bacchis, o mea Bacchis, servatrix mea!
    BA. bene factum et volup est. **PAM**. factis ut credam facis,
    antiquamque adeo tuam venustatem obtines,
    ut voluptati obitus, sermo, adventus tuos, quoquomque adveneris,
860   semper siet. **BA**. at tu ecastor morem antiquom atque ingenium obtines,
    ut unus hominum homo te vivat numquam quisquam blandior.
    PAM. hahahae, tun mihi istuc? **BA**. recte amasti, Pamphile, uxorem
        tuam;
    nam numquam ante hunc diem meis oculis eam, quod nossem, videram:
    perliberalis visast. **PAM**. dic verum. **BA**. ita me di ament, Pamphile!
865   **PAM**. dic mi, harunc rerum numquid dixti iam patri? **BA**. nil.
        PAM. neque opus est
    adeo muttito. placet non fieri hoc itidem ut in comoediis,
    omnia omnes ubi resciscunt. hic quos par fuerat resciscere
    sciunt; quos non autem aequomst scire neque resciscent neque scient.
    BA. immo etiam qui hoc occultari facilius credas dabo.
870   Myrrina ita Phidippo dixit iureiurando meo
    se fidem habuisse et propterea te sibi purgatum. **PAM**. optumest;
    speroque hanc rem esse eventuram nobis ex sententia.

Bacchis) But there's Bacchis standing in front of the door. **(855)** She's waiting for me, I expect. I'll approach. *(Goes up to her and takes her by the hands)*

BACCHIS: Hello, Pamphilus.

PAMPHILUS: Oh Bacchis, my own dear Bacchis, my saviour!

BACCHIS: No trouble - it's a pleasure.

PAMPHILUS: Your actions convince me of that, and you're still as lovely as ever. It's always a pleasure to see you, listen to you, meet you, no matter where. **(860)**

BACCHIS: And, upon my soul, *you* still have *your* old character and ways. There's not a man alive more captivating than yourself.

PAMPHILUS: Ha ha, you can say that to me?

BACCHIS: You did right to fall in love with your wife, Pamphilus. To the best of my knowledge I'd never seen her for myself before today, but she seems very much a lady.

PAMPHILUS: Come now, the truth.

BACCHIS: Heaven preserve me, Pamphilus, that is the truth! **(865)**

PAMPHILUS: *(Drops his voice)* Then tell me: you haven't mentioned any of this to her father, have you?

BACCHIS: Not a word.

PAMPHILUS: No need to either - not so much a a whisper. I'd rather this weren't like in the comedies where everyone finds out about everything. In the present case those who have a right to find out already know; while those who shouldn't know won't find out and won't work it out for themselves.

BACCHIS: Yes, and what's more, I'll tell you something to make it easier for you to believe the secret can be kept: **(870)** Myrrina has told Phidippus she's accepted the assurance I gave and that therefore you've been cleared in her eyes.

PAMPHILUS: Wonderful, and I hope everything turns out as we want it. *(Bacchis returns to her house)*

PAR. ere, licetne scire ex te hodie quid sit quod feci boni?

aut quid istuc est quod vos agitis? PAM. non licet. PAR. tamen
suspicor:

875 ego hunc ab Orco mortuom, quo pacto...? PAM. nescis, Parmeno,
quantum hodie profueris mihi et ex quanta aerumna extraxeris.

PAR. immo vero scio, neque inprudens feci. PAM. ego istuc satis scio.

PAR. an
temere quicquam Parmeno praetereat quod facto usu' sit?

PAM. sequere me intro, Parmeno. PAR. sequor. equidem plus hodie
boni

880 feci inprudens quam sciens ante hunc diem umquam. plaudite!

PARMENO: *(Puzzled)* Master, would you mind actually telling me just what the good turn that I've done is, and what it is you two are talking about?

PAMPHILUS: No, I won't.

PARMENO: I can guess though. *(Rubs his chin in puzzlement)* **(875)** I brought him back from Hell, dead as he was: how?

PAMPHILUS: Parmeno, you don't know how much you've done for me today and from what anguish you've rescued me.

PARMENO: *(Feigning understanding)* Ah, but I do know; I wasn't acting in the dark.

PAMPHILUS: *(With heavy irony)* I'm sure that's so.

PARMENO: Would Parmeno be so careless as to overlook anything that needed doing?

PAMPHILUS: Follow me inside, Parmeno.

PARMENO: I am doing. At all events, I've done more good today **(880)** without knowing it than I ever knowingly did before. *(He turns to the audience)* Give your applause.

Apparatus Criticus

Didascalia

I.   5 Apollodoru *Don. Praef. I,1*,
         6 data secundo *post* prologo *habet A om. Fleckeisen*, acta...secundo *del.*
Dziatzko.

II.   1 Megalensibus C^1, Romanis FEC^2L
         3 tota *post* peracta *habent* FEC^2L
         4 tota:totam *PDp, om. cett.*

Periocha

1 duxit Σ

3 eiusque Σ

Text

2 nova *codd.* novae *edd.* "deest huic" *Don.*

7 *lacunam post hunc versum statuunt edd.*, possit *codd.* posset *Don. Bentley.*

34 *versum del. multi.*

43 nulla γD^2L, non *cett.*

58 paucis *Don.* "sic enim Apollodorus".

64 misereas *A*, misereat P^1C^1 *Don. Lindsay-Kauer*, te misereat *DLpEF*.

69 voluntatem *D*.

88sq Syrae dat C^1.

97 quae γD *Don.* "qualia scilicet et quanta", quod *A*.

106 amabunt p^1 *Don.*, ament *A*, bene ament *cett.*

134 perduint *APCED*, perdent p^2F^1, faxint *conj. Bentley*, perdant *Dziatzko*. isto
odio *PCE Marouzeau*, istoc odio D^1p *Lindsay-Kauer*, odio isto *A*.

150 *versum post 151 posuit Fleckeisen.*

160 atqui AD^1pE *Don.* "legitur et atque", atque *cett. Lindsay-Kauer.*

167 animus *codd.*, animi *Dziatzko*, animo *Fleckeisen.*

169 huc *A*, huic γDL.

174 reliquit γD^2L *Lindsay-Kauer*, relinquit AD^1 *Don.* "legitur et reliquit",
Marouzeau.

177 primo *Jov.* D^1p^1, primos *A*, primum γ.

201 *del. Bentley*, oderunt oderunt *Umpfenbach.*

205 hem *initio v. 206 scribit Marouzeau.*

206 bene *om.* $A\gamma D^1$.

208 scio *Sostratae dant Bentley Fleckeisen Marouzeau*, Lacheti *codd. Lindsay-
Kauer.*

220 est *om.* γD^2L.

258 etsi *om. Don. Lindsay-Kauer.*

260 magni facere *Jov. CPLp^1*. magnificare *cett.*

277 expurgatu *APCE,* excusatu *F^1.*

280 exspecto *codd. Don.,* expeto *Bentley.*

283 hui *Fleckeisen, Lindsay-Kauer,* cui *codd.*

288 at sic *L^{2}PE Marouzeau, cf. Don.* "sed sic", ac sic *A Lindsay-Kauer.*

295 *post 296 Σ.*

306 haud *codd. Don.,* aut *Bentley.*

307 non maxumae...iniuriae *Bentley.*

315 trepidari...sensistin *Parmenoni dant* γ, agedum...propius *Pamphilo dat D.*

316 accede *codd. praeter AD^{1}p,* em sensistin *Parmenoni dant DLp.*

320 celant γ*D^{2}L^{1}p^2 Lindsay-Kauer,* celas *cett. Marouzeau.*

360 veniant *A,* redeant *Σ.*

370 illic *p,* illuc *P^{1}D,* illis *cett.*

378 exieram *Dziatzko,* extra eram *Fleckeisen.*

393 ait *Fielitz,* eam *post* concubuisse *habent codd. praeter A.*

393-4 *versus del. Dziatzko.*

406 data *Don.,* bona *codd.*

408 huc *Lindsay-Kauer,* nunc huc *Jov. C^1,* nunc huic *cett.,* huic nunc *Marouzeau,* huic *Umpfenbach.*

430 *post* etiam nunc *habent codd., del. edd.*

453 LA: nescio quem *Dziatzko.*

455 ipsus...tecum *Lacheti dant* γ*D, Phidippo cett.*

468 modo *p,* omnia *AD^1,* omnia modo *cett.*

478 quae *Jov.,* cui *cett.*

487 quod vellem meritam *DpF,* id quod v. m. *A,* m.q.v. *cett.,* m.i.q.v. *Marouzeau.*

493 *totum versum Lacheti dat Jov.*

495 mane γ*D^{2}L,* ades *A Marouzeau.*

524 sim *Ap,* sum *cett.*

543 omnibus *post* id *habent codd., del. Bentley.*

555 ducerem *A,* dicerem *D^{2}LEF^2.*

576 sciat *A.*

579 exoptem *AD^{1}p,* opto *CPEL,* exopto *cett. Marouzeau.*

603 induces *A,* inducas *Σ.*

604 illa *edd.,* illam *codd. Don.,* itaque <ea> u.e.ego illam *Marouzeau.*

617 concordes magis *AD^{1}F Bentley Marouzeau,* magis *om. CP^{1}ED^{2}L,* si non *codd.* non *om. Marouzeau,* non *ante* credo *posuit Dziatzko.*

618 nescias *Σ,* nescio *A.*

620 fabulae *codd.,* fabula *Faber Guyet.*

628 aperiam *codd. Don.,* operiam *Bentley.*

633 mutatio fit *Pamphilo dat Jov., Phidippo codd.*

643 natum illum et tibi i.s. δ *praeter L Marouzeau,* natum tibi i.s. *Jov. Lindsay-Kauer,* natum filium et tibi i.s. *A,* natum illum tibi et i.s. γ*L.*

656 sese *A Lindsay-Kauer,* se esse *Jov.* Σ *Marouzeau.*

657 quae *CPD¹p¹,* quem *LD²p²F.*

661 est Σ, siet *A Lindsay-Kauer (del.* ne).

667 *ante 666 posuit Bothe.*

670 ipsa *D¹p Don.*

688 690 del. *Dziatzko om. Fleckeisen.*

704 tollent Σ, tollet *A.*

709 mea *post* uxor *habent codd.*

721 et Σ, at *A.*

736 dicis *A*γ, dices *Dp Marouzeau.*

739 si facis *A,* si id nunc facis Σ.

740 me *post* tibi Σ, *om. A Don.* "inscitum me scilicet".

746 amicum *post* firmiorem *habent* γ*D², ante* firmiorem *A.*

765 facies *AD¹p,* facias *cett.*

779 falso *post* uxor *habent* γ*D².*

787 ego *D¹pE,* ergo *cett. Marouzeau.*

790 *om. Fleckeisen Phillimore,* 789-90 del. *Dziatzko.*

791 *versus deest in A, post 783 posuerunt Dp,* PH. *om.*γ*L, versum Bacchidi dat D.*

798 referet *AD Lindsay-Kauer,* referetque γ*D²L,* refert *Bentley,* iunget *EP²F² Lindsay-Kauer,* iungit *AC Marouzeau.*

826 id *D¹p, om. cett.*

830 habente *Bentley,* habentem *codd.*

845 dixe *Bentley,* dixisse *codd.*

849 qui donem *D¹p,* quid donem *cett.,* qui qui *D¹p¹E² Lindsay-Kauer,* quid qui *LE¹F,* quid quid *AC.*

853 ignavom *A,* ingratum Σ.

861 hominum Σ *Lindsay-Kauer,* omnium *A Marouzeau.*

865 iam Σ, meo *A.*

866 placet...*Bacchidi dant* Σ.

877 an...*Pamphilo cont. Ap¹, Bacchidi dat Don.*

Commentary on the Translation

Production Notice

Found in two clearly related forms: the longer in A, the oldest surviving manuscript, the second, shorter version in the other manuscripts of Terence. It has been traditional to accept the information they provide as essentially authentic and to see it as derived ultimately from some lost work - perhaps the *De Actis Scaenicis* - of Varro, the great Roman scholar of the first century B.C. who was presumably able to draw upon such contemporary official material as the *Commentarii Aedilium* and the records of actor-managers. Subsequent transmission and accretion, however, have clearly resulted in corruption and confusion.

Notice 1

1 The Megalensian Games: Held annually during April in honour of Cybele, the Great (Gk. *megale*) Mother Goddess of Asia Minor whose cult image was brought to Rome in 205-4 B.C.
2 Sextus Julius Caesar and Gnaeus Cornelius Dolabella: Curule Aediles in 165 B.C. Their office was the lowest magistracy in Rome to confer upon its holders entry into the Senate and though not an essential part of the *cursus honorum*, the progressive offices of Roman political life, its association with the Megalensian and Roman Games rendered it a ready means of gaining popular support and favour by the politically ambitious; for although the expense of the Games was in large measure defrayed by the state, it was nevertheless expected that presiding magistrates would augment the opulence of the festival from their own resources. In addition to organising the Games, the Aediles also had charge of maintaining and regulating Rome's streets, traffic, water supply and markets, and of overseeing the provision and distribution of the city's corn supply.
4 double pipe: A reed instrument like the Greek *aulos*. It usually consisted of two pipes (in this instance equal in length) fixed to the player's mouth by a band which passed over the player's head, leaving both hands free to work the stops (Beare[2] p.168f., pl.VI, cf. Bieber fig. 541). Whether one pipe provided the melody while the other gave a variable drone-like accompaniment, or whether one somehow extended the range of the other is not clear (see further OCD *Music* 9 ii).
(slave): The most probable interpretation of the Latin grammar at this point, lit. "Flaccus *of/belonging to* Claudius". The Production Notices of the other plays make it clear that Flaccus was Terence's invariable choice as musician.

5 Menander: Both Donatus in *Praefatio I* of his commentary on the play and in his Appendix to Suetonius' Biography (Penguin *Terence* p.393f.) and Eugraphius in the preamble to his discussion of the prologues give the author more correctly as Apollodorus of Carystus, a writer of comedies in the first half of the third century B.C. who was reputedly much influenced by Menander (Webster p.225ff.).

fifth play: There is a problem here. Following the modern *communis opinio* on the chronology of Terence's plays (see <u>Introduction</u> p.2) it clearly becomes impossible to take the information given by the Production Notice at face value. As a result we must posit either that the figure V, found in MS A and echoed by Donatus, is wrong (Carney), or that it refers to the second failed presentation at the funeral games for Aemilius Paulus in 160 B.C. and ignores the first production in 165 (Ashmore p.156; contrast, however, Flickinger[1] p.266, Beare[2] p.94, who place the second presentation of the play *after* that of *The Brothers*).

6 First staged without prologue: The statement has not won universal acceptance. Flickinger[1] p.235 n.4 argues that the preservation of two prologues suggests a *prima facie* assumption there never was a third. Bianco[1] p.179 on the other hand sees in the words simply an indication that the true first prologue had been lost by the time the Production Notice came to be written.

7 Lucius Aemilius Paulus: A prominent political and military figure during the first half of the 2nd century B.C. His second son, adopted into the Scipionic family as Scipio Aemilianus, has traditionally been regarded as the nucleus of a philhellenic grouping known as the Scipionic Circle, which is said to have included Terence in its number (see further Suetonius' Biography of Terence: Penguin *Terence* p.389ff., Goldberg p.13 who argues cogently against the existence of such coteries).

11 Lucius Ambivius Turpio: The actor-manager and producer of all Terence's plays, still remembered as a famous actor in the time of Cicero (*De Senectute* 48) and Tacitus (*Dialogus de Oratoribus* 20.3).

Lucius Sergius: Otherwise unknown. His presence in the Production Notice, like that of L. Hatilius Praenestinus in each of Terence's other plays or the association of L. Minucius Prothymus with *Adelphoe* (and *Eunuchus* according to Donatus), may refer to a later restaging of the play, details of which have been subsumed into the record of *Hecyra*'s third performance (Garton p.263), but any certainty is impossible. Further complication arises from the insertion of the name actually within that of Ambivius. The cause may be no more than textual corruption, or it may indicate that the name Turpio was common to both men.

Notice 2

Despite the more abbreviated form of Notice 2 compared with that found in A, the overall similarity of information given, not least the order of presentation, suggests the two derive from a common manuscript archetype.

Summary

Gaius Sulpicius Apollinaris: The author of short summaries attached to each of Terence's plays and tutor to both the ill-fated emperor Pertinax (murdered in A.D. 193) and the writer Aulus Gellius. The summaries themselves are of little importance to any appreciation of the plays, providing no more than a resumé of antecedents to the action and a description of the major events portrayed.

4 courtesan: See 58f. n., *mistresses*.
5 without having consummated: Though the text nowhere specifically refers to consummation of the marriage between Pamphilus and Philumena, its occurrence is implicit in 169 & 393.

Characters

Unlike the manuscripts of Greek plays, those of the Roman comic playwrights do not include lists of the characters involved in the action, though it has become traditional to reconstruct them in editions from the MSS scene headings, where the names of speakers are given. New Comedy, especially in its Greek form, emphasised its strong tendency towards the presentation of stock characters by making repeated use of the same names for similar roles in different plays, assisted in this no doubt by a similar reliance upon stock masks (Sandbach[2] p.63f.). On occasion the choice of a name might also indicate a trait of character, though generally the Greek theatre never went as far as Plautus was later to do in employing names, often of a fantastical construction, for specifically comic effect: Misargyrides ("Son of Money-hater"), the money-lender in *Mostellaria*, or Peniculus ("Sponge"), the parasite of *Menaechmi*. Terence himself returned to a position more akin to that of the Greek originals, and while not slavishly following his models by adopting without alteration the names they employed, nevertheless restricted himself to more conventional forms. Some of these in *The Mother-in-Law* do, however, display a certain degree of appropriateness: the *phil* element of Philotis, Pamphilus and Philumena, for instance, clearly points to the emotional attachment of love, just as Parmeno suggests in its Greek root (*parameno*) a character who stays close at hand, and as such is well suited to an ostensible confidant, ever-ready to share his master's troubles (cf. Parmeno in *The Eunuch*). The remaining characters on the other hand possess names that are for the most part simply appropriate to their social position. Thus Laches and Phidippus suggest little more than middle-class respectability (*pace* Austin p.82ff.); while of the women Sostrata (a female version of 'saviour of the army') is merely a name of good omen (cf. *The Self-Tormentor, The Brothers*), and Myrrina one conventionally given to respectable married women in New Comedy (Menander's *Dyskolos, Georgos, Perikeiromene*, Plautus' *Casina*), just as Bacchis, with its connotations of bacchic licence, was frequently found associated with the 'courtesan' type in both comedy and real life (*The Self-Tormentor, The Brothers*, Austin p.89). Of the remaining characters Syra ('Syrian woman') is no more than an ethnic slave name, though Sosia, with its connotations of saving, does fit with ironic aptness the 'faithful' slave who has survived the perils of travel by sea with his master. Among other names mentioned Scirtus, with its overtones of 'jumping to it', likewise suits the slave-type, just as the aristocratic formation Callidemides ('Son of a fair district') is clearly fabricated by Pamphilus at 432 for its ability to impress. Despite the semantic potential of such names, however, the actual extent to which a Roman audience was able to grasp their inner significance as opposed to their conventional implications for character type, must remain open to question.

Prologue I

Delivered on the occasion of the second presentation, at the funeral games of Aemilius Paulus in 160 B.C. Unlike Plautus, in whose plays the prologue speaker, if at times not actually characterised, nevertheless remained firmly embedded in the comic ambience of the occasion, Terence never made any attempt to incorporate his own prologue speakers into the dramatic illusion of the plays. They exist instead simply to act as spokesmen in his attempts to counter either the vagaries of his Roman audiences or the attacks of Luscius Lanuvinus. In contrast to the prologues found elsewhere in Terence, the first prologue of *The Mother-in-Law* exhibits a remarkable brevity. So brief is it in fact that commentators have been tempted to postulate either a loss of lines in the course of textual transmission (see below 6f. n.) or its complete spuriousness. That the prologue is both intact and inherently symmetrical as it stands, however, is well demonstrated by Goldberg p.37ff.

1f. When first staged: In April 165 B.C., as the Production Notices indicate. The opening lines of the play show immediately Terence's liking for the insertion of word-play and alliteration, especially important here at the beginning, where they could form a useful means of capturing and holding the audience's attention: *nova, novom*, lit. "When *newly* staged...by a *new* inauspicious event", cf. *studio - stupidus* 4, *iterum - iterum* 7, *cognostis - noscite* 8, *orator - ornatu - exorator* 9f., *iure - iure* 10f., *senem - adulescentior* 10f., *novas - inveterascerent* 12, *partim - partim* 15, *incerta - certum* 17, *easdem - eodem* 18, *studiose - studio* 19, *otio - negotio* 26, *calamitas - calamitatem* 30f., *vostra - nostrae* 31f., *vetere - nova* 37, *loco - locum* 41f., *datumst - datur* 44, *auctoritas - auctoritati* 47f., *maxumum - maxume* 50f., *inique - iniqui* 54, *causa - causam* 55 (see further Marouzeau[2] I p.225 n.2, II p.118 n.5). Needless to say it is often impossible to repeat the effect in translation; nor indeed would modern sensibilities appreciate the frequency of such word-play or the studied rhetoric that is likewise evident in much of the prologues.

2 inauspicious event: Terence's use of *vitium* here is taken from the practice of augury, where the word signified an event of ill-omen preventing the commencement of proceedings or interrupting them once begun.

4 all agog with eagerness: The alliteration of *studio stupidus* highlights an unflattering description of the audience. The implication of the references here and at 33f. is that the failure of the play at its first presentation was caused not through any inherent fault but by the audience's expectation of, and enthusiasm for, the spectacle of a tight-rope walker, which effectively prevented the actors from making any progress.

5 by way of a new play: Terence's wording, *pro nova*, implies recognition by the author that the earlier attempted production prevents him from claiming the second presentation as a totally new work, hence Donatus' comment *ad loc.* "for it is not now a new play", cf. Eugraphius *ad loc.* "it returns as if a new play". The initial failure on the other hand had evidently left open the possibility of subsequent staging on the grounds that the play had not been seen in its entirety.

6f. its author...second time: The phrasing of these lines has produced considerable uncertainty as to Terence's meaning. Some recent commentators, inspired perhaps by Donatus' observation *ad. loc.*: "Why then was the play not restaged once the tight-rope walker had finished? Was it because the poet preferred to represent himself as greedy for money rather than lacking in confidence in his own work?", have suggested after 7 a loss of lines in which the real reason for not restaging the play was supposedly given: i.e. "its author didn't wish...just so he could...a second time (but because...)". More likely, however, 6-7 simply indicate in a semi-jocular form the playwright's assertion of the work's inherent quality: his motive in restaging the work was *not* profit.

Prologue II

Delivered on the occasion of the third presentation in 160 B.C. The speaker, instead of being the usual minor member of the company of actors (cf. *The Self-Tormentor* 2), is now the producer and principal actor himself, Ambivius Turpio, employing all the authority and popularity gained through a lifetime in the theatre to win the audience's favour, much as he had earlier done in the case of *The Self-Tormentor*, Terence's next production after the ill-fated first attempt to stage *The Mother-in-Law* in 165. Gone is the tart brevity of the first prologue; instead the audience is wooed by memories of past collaboration with Ambivius to ensure the plays of Caecilius found the success they deserved, and invited to grace the present festival with appropriate fair-minded decorum. Such personal references to the role of the producer both here and in *The Self-Tormentor* invite indeed the question whether composition of the prologues owed more to Ambivius himself than to Terence.

9 dressed as prologue-speaker: i.e. either not yet in the costume of the part he was subsequently to play, or without at least the character mask that would otherwise have hidden his true identity (Flickinger[1] p.268. On the vexed question of masks in Roman Comedy see Duckworth[2] p.92ff., Beare[2] p.184ff. 303ff., Bieber p.154ff., Sandbach[2] p.111f., Gow).

to plead a case: lit. "as an orator", underlining the oratorical nature of the second prologue with its balance of syntax and phrasing (see above 1f. n.).

12 when I caused...favourites: An obvious attempt to associate Terence's recent difficulties with those experienced for whatever reason by earlier playwrights, whose works Ambivius had ultimately vindicated, and through such association to suggest that *The Mother-in-Law* was equally deserving of success. The reference to plays becoming "established favourites" implies not only that the restaging of popular plays could be a frequent occurrence, but also that such popularity might be due as much to the skill of the producer and his company as to the intrinsic merits of the plays themselves. At *The Self-Tormentor* 43-5 Ambivius had complained wearily in fact that he was often approached when the play to be presented was a difficult one, whereas easier works went to other companies. (On the repetition of plays see Plautus *Casina* 5-20, Duckworth[2] p.65ff. Donatus in a note on *Eunuchus* Praefatio I 6, records that this particular play was so successful it was repeated - Suetonius says on the same day - and earned the unprecedented sum of 8,000 sesterces.)

14 Caecilius: Caecilius Statius, reputedly Rome's most popular comic playwright in the period immediately following the death of Plautus c.184 B.C. until his own death in 168 B.C. (see further Wright p.87ff., Duckworth[2] p.46ff., Beare[2] p.86ff.,

CHCL p.115f. The main ancient assessment of Caecilius' work is provided by Aulus Gellius II 23, cf. Varro *Menippean Satires* 399: "Caecilius takes first place for his plots, Terence for his characters, Plautus for his dialogue", and Horace Epistles II 1, 59: "Caecilius wins for his weighty tone, Terence for his skill". In the canon of comic writers produced by Volcacius Sedigitus at the end of the 2nd century B.C. and preserved in Aulus Gellius XV, 24, Caecilius similarly occupies first place compared to Plautus in second and Terence in sixth place. For the extant fragments of his plays see Warmington vol. I.)

Ambivius' introduction of Caecilius here is clearly designed not only to particularise the general statement in 12f., but more importantly to link him with Terence through the problems they both faced and their common association with Ambivius, and thus to claim for Terence the ultimate success that Caecilius had enjoyed. No less relevant to 160 B.C. is the allusion in 20f. to the older playwright's eventual triumph over adversity, just as the reference in 22f. to the ill-will of Caecilius' opponents almost driving him from his vocation has its counterpart in the activities of Luscius Lanuvinus, the "spiteful old poet" who figures in one form or another in each of Terence's plays: *The Mother-in-law* 47 & 54, *The Woman from Andros* 6f., *The Self-Tormentor* 22, *The Eunuch* 4ff., *Phormio* 1ff., *The Brothers* 1ff. (see further Garton p.41ff., Grimal).

24 But if...his works: Probably a reference to the producer rejecting a play referred to him by the Aediles, or offered to him directly by its author. In his biography of Terence Suetonius records the unlikely, though illuminating, anecdote of the young poet being instructed by the Aediles to recite his play *Andria* to the aged Caecilius before they would accept it. At first the shabbily dressed young playwright was treated coolly, but after hearing a few lines of the play Caecilius was so impressed he invited Terence to join him at dinner.

30 in silence: That Roman audiences could be noisy is clear not only from the evidence of the present play but also from the more comically exaggerated description of Plautus at *Poenulus* 11-35.

31 your good sense: Like 44f. part of the *captatio benevolentiae*, the attempt to secure the favour of the audience by means of flattering its powers of discernment.

33 talk of a boxing-match: Despite alternative interpretations by Ashmore ("some well-known boxers" or "the fame of some boxers") and Sargeaunt ("the vaunting of pugilists"), this would seem to be the most likely interpretation of the Latin, *pugilum gloria* (cf. Cicero *De Inventione* II 166: "*Gloria* means constant talk about someone (or something) mingled with praise", Lindsay[2]). Why, though, do we find no mention of the boxing match in the first prologue? Did it in fact occur? If it did, is the omission a sign that Terence five years later had determined to depreciate the audience's lack of taste in the first prologue by concentrating on the less esteemed display of a tight-rope walker (Sandbach[3] p.135)? And had he

108

subsequently learned better than to scold the very people he ultimately relied upon
for the success of his plays so that in the second prologue he turned instead to
emphasise (by fabrication if necessary) the purely external factors he now claimed
as the cause of earlier failure?

35 crowds of supporters: The most probable translation for the Latin here: the
rumour of a boxing match at the same venue as Terence's play resulted in a sudden
influx of supporters, causing uproar as they scrambled for places and doubtless
reacting with less than sympathy at being faced with a mere Terentian comedy.

the screaming of women: Their reaction to the sudden arrival of crowds of new
spectators.

39 In the first part: Without doubt the correct interpretation of the Latin *primo
actu* rather than the more apparently obvious "in the first Act". So far as we can
judge from the extant remains of Menander's works, Greek New Comedy had
continued the tradition of the previous century by including choral intervals in the
plays: four intervals dividing the action into five episodes. The fact that the text of
these has not survived, however, and they are marked in the plays simply by the
term "(performance) of the chorus", a practice already beginning to be seen at
points in Aristophanes' last two surviving plays, *Ecclesiazusae* of 393 B.C. and
Plutus of 388, suggests that by Menander's time they had ceased to have any
relevance to the action and were retained simply as a convention. In the context of
Rome, lacking as it did a history of choral presentation, such intervals clearly made
no sense, hence their omission from the plays of both Plautus and Terence (with
the exception perhaps of Plautus' *Pseudolus* 573f.), and their replacement, certainly
in the works of Plautus, by song from the stage characters themselves. Without
choral intervals the division of Roman comedy into Acts thus becomes an artificial
imposition of form onto the plays, which available evidence suggests were written
for continuous uninterrupted performance. That Act divisions are in fact found in
the MSS and go back to antiquity but perhaps only to the 1st century B.C. to judge
from the reference to Varro by Donatus (*Hecyra* Praefatio III 6), in no way
invalidates our conclusion. Donatus himself in fact describes the difficulty
encountered in attempting to divide Terence's works into Acts at *Andria* Praefatio
II 3 and *Eunuchus* Praefatio I 5.

45 you the opportunity...festivals: Like 31f. part of the *captatio benevolentiae*
designed to secure the audience's favour by suggesting its attention to the
proceedings will grace the whole festival.

47 the hands of only a few: A scarcely veiled reference to Luscius Lanuvinus and
his clique, cf. the "unjust individuals" of 54.

49ff. If I...interests: By stressing that his first consideration has never been
personal gain but rather that the plays he presents to his audiences should always
be of the highest quality Ambivius reminds his audience of the debt owed to him in

return. His words indeed hark back to the theme developed in 12ff.: that Ambivius has not limited himself in the past simply to presenting plays that were sure of success but has attempted instead to educate the audience's taste by persisting with plays in which he recognised indications of quality despite initially unfavourable reactions. Through this Ambivius forges another link between Caecilius, who came eventually to be placed in the forefront of comic writers, and Terence, whose own play is now held up as similarly deserving of distinction.

53 entrusted...himself to...fair-dealing: By hinting at the client-patron relationship Ambivius seems set on inducing the audience to accept the existence of such a relationship between themselves and Terence, and hence their responsibility for defending their client against his detractors by giving his play an uninterrupted and fair hearing.

54 unjustly derided: A reference perhaps to the charges of *contaminatio*, plagiarism, reliance on his friends, and the poor quality of Terence's writings which figure in the prologues to the other plays (see Introduction p.3).

57 purchased at my own expense: Our general ignorance of the process by which a play reached the stage makes the exact significance of the Latin here uncertain. Ambivius' statement and his reference earlier in the prologue to staging Caecilius' plays in order to secure others from him suggests speculative purchase by a producer who then hoped to recoup his outlay from the festival's presiding magistrates. At *The Eunuch* 20 on the other hand Terence mentions direct purchase by the Aediles, while Donatus in a note on *The Mother-in-Law* 57 suggests the producer's role was that of a middle-man: "If after my appraisal of how much the Aediles might pay and similarly my assessment of the work, it fails, the Aediles may seek to recover from me personally the price they paid to the poet." The result, we have to admit, is confusion, and in the case of *The Mother-in-Law*'s third production we cannot even be sure any normal procedure was followed. After the earlier failures Ambivius may well have undertaken the final production as a purely speculative venture on a point of honour.

(I i)

58-75 Philotis Syra: The entry of two women onto the stage (most likely, in view of 97f., from one of the three doors portrayed) introduces the first stage of exposition, the process by which in this and the following scene the audience is provided with those salient details of background information that form the basis of the plot; hence, as in the prologue, the almost exclusive use until 197 of the spoken iambic senarius metre for clarity and ease of comprehension. Technically both Philotis and Syra are *protatic* characters, i.e. brought into the action at its outset to establish the setting and prompt the disclosure of information, but who thereafter disappear never to be seen again. Such characters as a means of exposition had long been a standard feature of ancient drama: in Menander's *Dyskolos* for instance revelation of Sostratos' emotional attachment to Knemon's daughter is prompted on a human level by the questions of Chaireas. In Plautus we see them developed as a source of comic effect in their own right: Grumio in *Mostellaria*, Thesprio in *Epidicus* or Acanthio in *Mercator*. In Terence the protatic character reappears as Sosia in *Andria* and Davus in *Phormio*, but unlike their Plautine counterparts these emphasise more their primary function of eliciting information. The use of protatic characters in *The Mother-in-Law* is not, however, without an element of sophistication. The very fact that there are two of them allows an initial interaction and character differentiation: Syra the hard-bitten mercenary type, Philotis more open and ready to trust her clients. Not surprisingly it is the latter who interacts with Parmeno in the following scene and is the initial source of information concerning Bacchis, something Donatus in a note on 58 suggests may be anticipatory of later developments: "we should notice in this play how in order that his intention to introduce a good *meretrix* (see below 58f. n.) does not seem untoward, Terence brings on another good instance of the type". In addition, the division of exposition between two scenes mirrors the involvement of two characters, Pamphilus and Bacchis, in the initial situation, the latter represented by Philotis who first sets out the state of things from her own viewpoint, the former soon to be represented by his slave Parmeno. As often, the dialogue is given an additional air of naturalness by the impression that we come across the pair in mid-conversation.

58f. how very few lovers: Donatus *ad loc.* notes the variant reading already in existence by his day: "to how very few mistresses you find their lovers turn out faithful" and cites as corroborating evidence the original line by Apollodorus:

> ὀλίγαις ἐραστὴς γέγον' ἑταίραισιν, Σῦρα,
> βέβαιος.

"to few mistresses is a lover faithful, Syra". That Terence did, however, write "how very few lovers" is suggested by the subsequent concentration of Philotis' remarks of criticism upon Pamphilus, whom she evidently expected to be an exception to the rule.

mistresses: The Latin term *meretrix*, which translates the Greek *hetaira*, lit. "female companion", possesses far wider connotations than can be conveyed by any current English term, certainly wider than the often used translation 'prostitute' or 'courtesan'. Within the context of Roman comedy such characters might range from the helpless slave-girl totally in the power of a pimp and hired out for sex, to free non-citizen women who, though debarred from contracting a legal marriage with a citizen, were nevertheless able to attract and retain the devotion of well-to-do lovers by virtue of their intellectual and artistic accomplishments. Thais in Terence's *The Eunuch* is one such example. Equally, they might range from young girls genuinely in love - Philaenium in Plautus' *Asinaria* or Philematium in *Mostellaria* - to more mature types, soured by the experiences described by Scapha at *Mostellaria* 194ff. or Syra here at 63ff., for whom the financial side of any relationship was paramount, cf. Phronesium in Plautus' *Truculentus* or Bacchis in Terence's *The Self-Tormentor*. That Bacchis in *The Mother-in-Law* and Thais in *The Eunuch* depart from the general picture was noted by Donatus in an observation on *The Eunuch* 198: "he introduces well worn character types in a novel manner...so that when for instance he makes a *meretrix* good, he captivates and charms the minds of his audience".

65 take him...rob him blind: The sentiments, which aptly and succinctly sum up the cynical and grasping character of Syra, are further reinforced by their triadic structure and by the asyndeton and terminal assonance of the Latin: *spolies, mutiles, laceres*, cf. Caesar's *veni, vidi, vici* (Duckworth[2] p.341ff., Palmer p.92f.).

(I ii)

76-197 Parmeno Philotis Syra: The appearance of Parmeno through another of the stage doors ushers in the main expository scene of the play. As often elsewhere the abruptness of his unheralded entry is masked by his continuing to address an unseen character indoors (cf. *The Woman from Andros* 481-5, 684f., *The Brothers* 209f., 511-6, 635f., 787f., Duckworth[2] p.125f.), a device which readily serves also to identify him as a slave through what he says. In the dialogue that follows the audience is first given a more detailed and explicit account of the rupture in relations between Pamphilus and Bacchis caused by the young man's marriage. It reverses in fact the implications of Philotis' opening statement - that the marriage was something of a betrayal of Bacchis - by showing not only that it was forced upon Pamphilus by his father, and as a result not at first accepted by him, but also that the actual breakdown in the affair appears to have been brought about by Bacchis herself through a radical change of attitude towards her lover. From this the report turns to Pamphilus' growing love for his young wife, his despatch to Imbros, and the mysterious rift which subsequently developed between her and her mother-in-law, resulting in the girl's return to her parental home and the arrival in town of Pamphilus' father in an effort to resolve the situation. Into the bare details of the narrative, however, Terence injects both motivation for their revelation - Philotis' absence from Athens for the last two years - and an element of characterisation which makes their disclosure all the more natural - Parmeno's penchant for gossip.

76 the old man: Laches, a conventional method of referring to an older master behind his back.

79f. If he doesn't ask...other time: In addition to injecting an element of general humour into the introduction of Parmeno, his opening speech also serves to set him within the ambit of the cunning slave character type. As such not only is he careful to ration information so that what he now does in reality may be used on some future occasion as an excuse when he wishes to head off in another direction for his own purposes, but he here lays the foundation for his later self-description as the one person his young master turns to for advice and help in the midst of problems.

81 Philotis: In the Latin a diminutive form of the name is used (cf. 89, 197), thereby expressing an element of endearment and establishing an immediate sympathetic connection between the two even before they come into real contact.

83 Good morning, Parmeno: Once contact between Philotis and Parmeno is established, Syra's role of providing an initial foil for her friend comes to an end. After her greeting here no more is heard either from her or of her, as the axis of attention swings to the other two. Suggestions, however, that she leaves the stage at this point (Gilula[2] p.529) or that the paucity of her role indicates she was no more than a mute in the Apollodoran version (Lowe p.437) are unnecessary. (On such characters in general see Prescott[1], Wilner[2].)

84 Tell me...time?: Just as a sympathetic use of Philotis' name in 81 ushered in the first contact between the two, so the motivation for her enquiries into recent developments is neatly introduced and guided by playful and ironic quips from Parmeno.

97 But what's going on?: Philotis' question signals the end of initial pleasantries and the introduction of important dramatic detail. In terms of real life it is of course illogical that she should have gathered so little clear or detailed information from Bacchis inside, but in terms of stage logic and the needs of the audience the vagueness of Philotis' knowledge proves essential since 1) by prompting the revelation of events from Parmeno it enables him to pose as something of a confidant to his master, and 2) it allows the information he provides and its implications to form the factual basis for subsequent dramatic action until his version is shown ultimately to be so ill-founded. In addition, Bacchis' failure to provide Philotis with more information accords well with the picture of her established towards the end of the play as a character who has her former lover's interests at heart, rather than the hard-hearted mercenary picture Parmeno draws.

108 *my* back: A reference to the punishment of whipping, frequently mentioned in Roman Comedy (Duckworth[2] p.288ff., Segal p.137ff.).

110f. As if...to my questions: A subtle piece of characterisation of Parmeno as the talkative slave, which serves as a useful escape from his recently voiced reluctance to engage in gossip. More importantly, however, it provides a partial motivation for the slave's later exclusion from any real understanding of the dilemma Pamphilus finds himself in as regards his wife's pregnancy, and points to the essential falseness of his role as confidant, a role to which he will shortly lay claim.

115ff. Pamphilus was just...: Donatus notes *ad loc.* that the whole of Parmeno's speech here is constructed as a defence of Pamphilus, to demonstrate that the breakdown of relations with Bacchis was the result of necessity not choice, and occasioned by circumstances beyond the control of either: the intervention of Laches (cf. 134 n.). Ironically Pamphilus' reluctance to give up his mistress is later to have positive repercussions from a most unlikely source, his father-in-law Phidippus, who sees in it at 554-6 an element of emotional stability.

117 the same old arguments all fathers do: In this way Laches' proposal, though unwelcome to his son and to those who sympathise with him, is shown to be unexceptional and hence all the more likely to succeed.

119 some security for his old age: Behind the assertion lies Laches' concern to ensure the physical continuity of his family through the birth of a grandchild, and specifically a male grandchild.

122 duty: Further evidence that Laches' suggestion and the arguments he introduces to advance it are not unreasonable in terms of ancient society; hence the initial weakening of Pamphilus' resistance through his recognition of the duty he owes his parents, which in turn serves to illustrate a positive aspect in his character. Dramatically, the dilemma Pamphilus here experiences as a reality - whether to follow his own emotions and maintain his relationship with Bacchis without the complicating factor of a wife, or whether to acknowledge his social responsibilities and agree to another woman sharing his life - serves as preparation for later developments, when family duty becomes both a reason and an excuse for his actions. The first of these manifests itself in his determination not to introduce a supposedly illegitimate child into the family, the latter in the use he makes of his mother to avoid taking back Philumena.

124 his next-door neighbour: Phidippus. On one level the choice of such a bride might be explained by Laches' knowledge of his neighbour's affairs and character. Essentially, however, it is a product of ancient stage convention and the convenience of having those involved in the action close at hand. The girl herself, Philumena, never appears onstage, though as Posani[1] p.229f. observes, she dominates the action by constantly occupying the minds of those characters we do see. Similarly there is no evidence in the text of Philumena being consulted as to whether she wished to marry Pamphilus, just as in Menander's *Dyskolos* neither Knemon's daughter nor Sostratos' sister is given any say in the matter of the husbands chosen for them. Marriage in antiquity was, after all, not a matter of personal preference born of emotional attachment but a formal agreement between two households involving a transfer of property in the form of dowry and aimed at the procreation of legitimate citizen offspring (MacDowell p.86ff., Harrison p.1ff., Fantham p.52). Preceding the marriage ceremony itself was the requirement of betrothal, such as Laches performs here, in which the bride-to-be was pledged to her future husband.

128f. Bacchis herself...would have pitied him: The depth of Pamphilus' predicament is graphically illustrated by Parmeno's suggestion that even the one person least likely to look with compassion on the situation would nevertheless have pitied him. The seriousness of Pamphilus' plight is further highlighted by 1) quotation of his actual words in 131-3, 2) the air of desperation and pleading seen in the repetition of Parmeno's name, and 3) the young man's agitation shown by the lack of connection between his brief staccato statements.

134 damn you, Laches: By directing Philotis' irritation against Laches rather than Pamphilus, as her statement 98ff. might have suggested, the playwright further reinforces the picture of the young man as victim of the situation, important if sympathy for him is not to be lost at this early stage. From this point on the role of Philotis declines to that of a typical Terentian protatic character - prompting the disclosure of information and by her interruptions breaking up into manageable sections what would otherwise have been a lengthy monologue from the slave with all its potential for tedium. At the same time her interruptions continue to steer the audience's own emotional reaction to what they hear in the direction the playwright requires.

135 he got married: lit. "he led his wife home", part of the final stage in a wedding ceremony.

136 he didn't touch the girl: Though by his description in 130ff. Parmeno has set himself up as privy to his master's affairs (cf. the emphasis on "in private" 144), this is the only confidential information he is allowed - crucial though it is for future developments (Sewart[3] p.257f., cf. Goldberg p.157f.). He knows nothing for instance of Philumena's true condition or its background, factors which, had they been given in an initial expository prologue, would have resulted in considerable dramatic irony at this point (see further 194 n.). For the time being, however, the audience is encouraged to accept him as the cunning-slave type whose inside and supposedly objective information will ultimately allow him to rescue his master from his predicament.

138f. A young man...off her?: Philotis' incredulity here not only highlights the unexpected nature of Pamphilus' behaviour after his marriage but also allows the playwright to emphasise its cause, the fact that he was an unwilling bridegroom. Elsewhere in New Comedy the ability of alcohol to inflame the passions of young men more usually served as both the cause of and excuse for sexual activity, especially rape (cf. Menander's *Epitrepontes* 471ff., Plautus' *Aulularia* 745, and the sexual innuendoes of Plautus' *Mostellaria* 313-35).

147 he'd hoped...marriage: Pamphilus' reaction to the prospect of married life goes through a number of stages: from shock at the inevitability of the wedding (131-3), to weak optimism that he might be able to reconcile himself to marriage (147), and finally to the realisation that such hopes were futile (148f.). Equally important for subsequent developments is his reaction to that realisation; for the way his rejection of married life is presented must not only retain the sympathy of the audience towards him (cf. 152), but must also ensure the credibility of his eventual transfer of affection to Philumena. Hence, when faced with a wife he never wanted and whom he feels he cannot keep, Pamphilus is pointedly made to examine in sequence the options open to him, and to reject those inimical to the ultimate aim of the action: 1) subjecting the girl to ridicule by keeping her in the sham role of wife and for this to become common knowledge - clearly unacceptable since it would reflect badly upon Pamphilus and would subject Philumena to the degradation of being the object of her husband's scorn and neglect; 2) sending Philumena back to her parents with her virginity intact - similarly unacceptable since it would be tantamount to public rejection of a girl by her husband in terms suggestive of divorce, but without any grounds to justify such an action; 3) for Philumena to leave of her own accord, presumably because of marital incompatibility. To Pamphilus it is this final possibility that offers the best hope for a satisfactory resolution of his predicament, a hope based, however, upon a negative tendency in his character to allow responsibility for events to settle onto the shoulders of others. In the present case Pamphilus hopes Philumena will rescue him from his difficulties; later he is to use first the supposed enmity between mother and wife, and then Philumena's concealment of the birth as excuses for not resuming marital relations. This theme of shirked responsibilities Terence was to return to in *The Brothers*, where Aeschinus' failure to reveal his relationship with Pamphila allows the development of considerable misunderstanding and anxiety, as Micio makes clear at 683-95.

149 to make her an object of ridicule: More literally "for her to be held up as a laughing-stock" (cf. 147 n.). The relationship of 149-51 ("it wouldn't be...parents") to Pamphilus' next statement at 153-5 ("I don't think...insolence") has caused difficulties for commentators, so much so that some have been tempted to accept Donatus' altogether untenable equation of "to make her an object of ridicule" with "rape". Instead, 153-5 merely repeats and extends the young man's rejection of keeping Philumena as a scorned wife before then rejecting the alternative, sending her back to her parents.

150 intact: What neither Pamphilus nor the audience realise at this point is that Philumena is no longer in fact a virgin. The potential for dramatic irony is therefore lost from the Roman viewpoint as a result of Terence's rejection of the expository prologue, as indeed it may well have been in the case of the Greek audience if Apollodorus employed a deferred prologue (see Introduction p. 10).

153 making the situation public: That Pamphilus cannot accept Philumena as his wife. The playwright here lays the foundation of what is later to prove an important factor in the development of the situation: the restriction of information to the minimum number of characters. Upon this ultimately lie the easy acceptance by Laches and Phidippus that the child was conceived in wedlock - allowing concentration instead to be focused on the themes of enmity and illness (see Appendix I, The Odium-Morbus Theme) - and the pressing need to dispense with Parmeno, whose intrusion into later scenes and swift despatch on patently false errands forms one of the few real sources of humour in the play.

157 Did he keep on visiting Bacchis?: Stavenhagen p.579 argues that the continued visits to Bacchis were necessary dramatically in order to make the theme of the marriage's non-consummation plausible. Rather, they serve to emphasise Pamphilus' refusal to accept that his newly married status had altered anything.

159 much harder...demands: While the accuracy of the information provided by Parmeno concerning his master's behaviour immediately after marriage is never called into question, there is considerable divergence within the play over the motivation behind Bacchis' own reaction to the situation. Here the audience is given a picture of the typical grasping *meretrix*, peeved at the evident duplicity of her lover and determined to make him pay, both emotionally and financially. Later, however, at 750ff. Bacchis' own account, together with her readiness to help resolve the difficulties between Pamphilus and his wife and the warmth of her interaction with him when they eventually meet (855ff.), all point to a far more positive and sympathetic figure. Instead of the harlot, we are there invited to see a woman who pointedly sacrifices her own interests for the sake of Pamphilus' marriage (756ff., 773ff., 833ff.). Parmeno's description in consequence becomes yet another aspect of his generally subjective and inaccurate assessment of the situation which he here offers as fact and upon which the action of the play is based (Sewart[3] p.254f.).

161 when Pamphilus took stock of himself: How did Parmeno acquire this information concerning his master's thought processes? Is the absence from the section of any direct quotation a signal by Terence that what Parmeno here offers as objective fact is in reality largely supposition on his part, or is it merely the playwright altering the manner of presentation for the sake of variety and economy?

165 unkind behaviour: McGarrity[1] p.35 points to the contrast of behaviour underlined by Terence's repetition of the Latin word *iniuria* here and in 168. In the first instance Philumena accepts unpleasantness without demur, thereby eventually preserving and strengthening her marriage; in the second Pamphilus refuses to accept similar treatment from Bacchis despite all his earlier protestations of loyalty (60ff.) and drifts away from her, a contrast of reaction that is heightened by the emphatic position the words occupy on both occasions at the end of their respective lines. The same basic term Terence had in fact employed for a similar contrasting effect in the opening scene of the play, 71f., where the repetition, translated as "wrong", highlighted the different approaches of Philotis and Syra to their profession. Significantly, it is Syra's vengeful, mercenary attitude that Parmeno now attributes to Bacchis herself. The difference of reaction between husband and wife that Terence paints here - Pamphilus the agent of injury, Philumena the victim who accepts - is to form indeed a *leitmotif* running through the whole play. Faced with the all too clear evidence of his wife's marred chastity, it is Pamphilus who acts, by refusing to take her back, and Philumena who must accept that decision for fear of even worse. Similarly we see it again at the very point of dénouement when Pamphilus, for all his earlier display of principles, is revealed as a rapist, while Philumena is the the victim no less of her husband's rape as of those same principles (cf. Fantham p.67ff.). In the context of the "unpleasantness", "unkind behaviour" and "insults" mentioned here Pamphilus' concern for Philumena's welfare at 148ff. begins to ring somewhat hollow. Has Terence allowed an element of inconsistency to creep into the account, or are the details given here indicative of the very methods Pamphilus employed to induce his wife to return home of her own accord, as he had hoped?

167f. partly...partly: Just as the process of Pamphilus' break with Bacchis was viewed through the balanced use of *iniuria*, so the transfer of emotion sees a similar balanced positioning of *partim* in 167 & 168 and the paronomasia (similar sound but contrasting meaning) of *devinctus* ("won over" lit. "bound") and *victus* ("worn down" lit. "overcome") in 168, which is further emphasised by the contrasted positioning of the two participles within their respective clauses.

170 a character like his own: Parmeno's observation serves not only to indicate the virtual inevitability of Pamphilus' change but also, by the reverse process, to introduce a further, if unspoken, blackening of Bacchis' character.

171 Imbros: An island in the N. Aegean opposite the Dardanelles which had once been subject to Athens, hence the presence there of one of Laches' relatives. More importantly for the action of the play, however, the island's remoteness from

Athens would ensure Pamphilus' absence from home long enough to cover the later stages of his wife's pregnancy.

172 by law his estate passed to them: For the legal consequences of any failure to produce direct heirs see Harrison p.122ff. esp. p.143ff., MacDowell p.92ff. esp. p.98f.

173 was packed off: The force of the expression, implying the need for the young man to be almost physically bundled out of the house, strengthens the sense of unwillingness with which he left the wife he had so recently grown to love.

174f. His wife...to town: The absence of Laches from the town house forms an essential prerequisite for the rift that supposedly developed between Sostrata and her daughter-in-law. Had he been present, we might have expected him to nip in the bud any dissension that arose. In addition, it is not by accident that Terence places the mention of mother and wife here, at the end of a lengthy section of narrative, immediately before the interruption by Philotis prompts the disclosure of further developments which lead in an altogether different direction from that already established. So far the whole tenor of Parmeno's account since 160 has been towards marital harmony, not the ramshackle affair mentioned in 101. Philotis' question at 176, therefore, is designed to return Parmeno to his original assertion and the problems of the present, as well as to break up what might otherwise have degenerated into a quasi-monologue. By including at the end of this section characters who form the centre of interest in the next, Terence is thereby able to use them to bridge Philotis' necessary interruption.

179 dislike: The first mention of what in a variety of guises is to become one of the major themes in the play (see Appendix I & 188 n.), supplying as it does either an explanation for the difficulties in which characters find themselves or a specious excuse by which they seek to avoid an even worse situation. Again the audience's ignorance of the truth removes the potential for dramatic irony here. Instead, Terence seems deliberately to deepen the mystery surrounding recent events by Parmeno's observation that this "strange dislike" failed to manifest itself through any of the usual symptoms of enmity.

181 So what was it?: Parmeno's narrative once again appears to be moving away from the theme of marital problems, hence Philotis' further interruption to correct its direction.

182f. disappear and refuse to see her: The outer manifestation of what Parmeno interprets as dislike. By careful control of the order in which information is supplied the playwright actually strengthens the audience's acceptance of what eventually proves a totally erroneous view. So for instance the conclusion Parmeno reaches is seen first as a hard fact (179). Only then comes the evidence for it, evidence which in other circumstances and with a different presentation might give rise to quite a different interpretation (cf. 159 n., 161 n. above).

185-93 The style adopted in these lines is remarkable for its lack of connectives and the general staccato effect, emphasising as it does the rapid breakdown of relations between the two families. Each stage in Sostrata's attempts to gain information about her daughter-in-law is pointedly designed to suggest dislike as its cause: first an excuse which Parmeno's description makes appear patently false, then no response at all, as if Philumena's family were not even attempting to maintain social contact, then the claim that the girl was ill, but only achieved after persistent enquiries and again suggestive of falsehood, as if it were offered only in an effort to stem enquiries, an interpretation seemingly confirmed by the subsequent refusal to allow Sostrata to see the girl.

188 the girl was ill: Like the theme of enmity or dislike (*odium*), 179, that of illness, *morbus*, runs like a thread through subsequent developments, advanced at times as a genuine explanation for events, on other occasions regarded as no more than an excuse. It is in this latter guise that Parmeno himself clearly takes it, and as Gilula[3] p.139ff. points out, insertion of the slave's interpretation amidst otherwise incontrovertible facts induces the audience to accept it as equally valid.

194 I'll be on my way: Returning the situation to 77, when Parmeno first appeared en route to the harbour. In this way Terence neatly rounds off the scene and offers foreshadowing of later events. Similarly, Philotis' reference to her date motivates her disappearance from both the stage and the play. That Syra also departed with her friend at this point has been the habitual conclusion of commentators (Prescott[2] p.197, Sewart[3] p.252 n.18), though lack of any reference to her in the text has also contributed to the view that Terence at times failed to visualise fully activity on the stage.

By this point in the action the audience has been given all the information it needs concerning previous events to allow the action proper to get underway. That this does not, however, include anything which as yet places it in a position of superiority over the characters on the stage and thus able to enjoy the dramatic irony inherent in the misapprehensions we eventually see them labouring under marks an important difference between Terence's approach to the plot and that characteristic of Greek New Comedy in general (see further Introduction p.10f.).

(II i)

198-242 Laches Sostrata: While identification of the two figures who now appear from one of the stage doors might have been achieved more easily and with greater economy by means of some introductory comment from Parmeno as he left the stage, Terence has chosen instead to allow the necessary information to emerge by more gradual and naturalistic means. To some extent the groundwork for identification has already been prepared: the final details of Parmeno's account, centred as they were on Sostrata's attempts to visit her daughter-in-law and the return of Laches from the country, invite the assumption of thematic continuity, while on a visual level the audience was probably aware of the couple's appearance through the same door as was earlier used by Parmeno himself. Similarly, the early reference in 201 to mothers-in-law and daughters-in-law invites identification of the couple as Pamphilus' parents.

Though thematically linked, the present scene nevertheless has no formal contact with what has gone before, an indication perhaps of the shift from revelation of past events to development of the present situation that was signalled in the original either by an Act division or by the ending of a deferred prologue. One result of this is the need to establish an immediate dramatic context for the scene, effectively achieved by the injection of a highly charged emotional atmosphere that stems from the almost exclusive use of long iambic octonarii until 216. These reinforce Laches' opening exclamations of general prejudice and anger, which serve in turn to characterise him from the outset as overbearing and insensitive. In a similar vein Sostrata's role as defendant becomes clear from her first words at 205, thereby neatly formulating the basis upon which the rest of the scene builds.

198-204: Laches' opening tirade, a fierce denunciation of the problems caused by women, exhibits a gradual progression from total generality, through the more specific categories of mothers- and daughters-in-law, to a conclusion with Sostrata herself.

202 opposing their husbands: Unlike the charge of women hating their daughters-in-law, this one is never given specific form; instead it springs from Laches' general low opinion of his wife, his belief that she cares nothing for all his hard work (224ff.), but does all she can to cause him additional worries.

205 I really can't imagine: A powerful indication of both the vagueness that marks Laches' outburst and, as Donatus observes *ad loc.*, Sostrata's innocence: she simply cannot understand what she has done to deserve the tirade launched against her, and hence cannot even begin a refutation of it. This is a perfectly understandable reaction at this point in the play, since according to Parmeno's account the only explanation Sostrata has actually been given concerning Philumena's failure to return to her marital home is based on illness.

206 Laches: As at 232, Sostrata's reference to her husband by name is designed to appeal to feelings of affection, in many respects a vain hope on her part, just as Laches' use of Sostrata's name in 223 seeks to use the same emotion to bolster his feelings of self-pity (contrast his stark use of "woman" in 214).

207 live out our lives together: The consistent gentleness of Sostrata's reaction to her husband's criticism contrasts strikingly with the unfeeling sentiments of

Laches, expressed as they often are in terms of blatant sarcasm. His jaundiced view owes nothing to the reality we see. Rather it is an offshoot of a misogynism which recurs throughout New Comedy in the relationships of elderly couples (Plautus' *Mercator* 556ff., *Mostellaria* 690ff., *Trinummus* 51ff.), and which characterises him as the insensitive and foolish old-man type (Goldberg p.153) whose hackneyed prejudices and ill-founded claims to human feelings (214), sacrifice of self (223ff.) and total grasp of the situation (217ff., cf. *The Brothers* 395ff.) will eventually reveal him as the character most out of touch with events. For the moment, however, the audience's lack of truly objective information only deepens the mystery of the situation as they listen to accusations in a context of character convention that only undermines their validity, yet know they essentially repeat and extend what has already been revealed by Parmeno.

210 disgrace on me...family: As with "my reputation among others" (218) it soon becomes clear that a major, if not the major, consideration in Laches' mind is his public image, hence his concern not to turn Phidippus and his family into enemies.

213 But single-handed: A final jibe, particularly effective, coming as it does after a long list of what Laches believes Sostrata has done.

214 You think...through: Donatus cites the original wording of Apollodorus:

σύ με παντάπασιν ἤγησαι λίθον

"You think I'm completely made of stone".

217-42: After the iambic octonarii with which the scene began the metre now changes to less volatile trochaic septenarii, much used by Terence for dialogue sections of his play, and thus more suitable and sustainable as Laches turns from outpourings of prejudice to specific complaints.

219 Some time ago: Laches' claim ill accords with the evidence provided by Parmeno in 190. There the slave had stated the old man returned from the country only the day before, which suggests either an element of exaggeration on Laches' part or that he is less concerned with the behaviour of his family than he claims - until a crisis arises.

taken a dislike to you: Only now does Laches actually begin to specify the precise nature of his complaint against Sostrata, advancing once again the *odium* theme of 179. Previously all we have heard from him has ranged from general bluster against women as a group, through crude insinuations of disbelief at Sostrata's confusion, blunt insults, and unspecified charges of bringing disgrace upon the family.

220 it's hardly surprising: A gratuitous slur, continuing as it does Laches' sour view of his wife with the implicit suggestion that Philumena's dislike for Sostrata was inevitable (cf. 240ff.).

222 *you* would have been sent packing: Laches' heartless threat foreshadows in a negative light Sostrata's later generous offer to sacrifice her own interests and the comforts of town-life by retiring to the country (586).

223 how undeserved this distress...is: Donatus notes *ad loc*. how Laches, true to type, turns from bitter denunciation to self-pity as he contrasts his own supposed hardships on the farm with the lifestyle he imagines the rest of his family enjoys as a result of his labours - and never a hint of gratitude. The dichotomy is further highlighted by the emphatic position of *te* ("you") and *mihi* ("me") at opposite ends of 227. The resentment Laches here feels against his family is later to resurface when he throws in Pamphilus' face his earlier forbearance over the affair with Bacchis (684f.).

232 I'm not saying that: Faced with her husband's charges yet unable to understand how she could have aroused her daughter-in-law's dislike, Sostrata at 228 had only been able to deny responsibility for the situation. In Laches' view, however, the charge is already proven: by attributing to Sostrata the same burden of responsibility for affairs in town as he has himself shouldered in the country, any alternative becomes unimaginable. Both his prejudice against Sostrata and his desire to maintain the link with Phidippus makes any thought of Philumena being to blame impossible. Hence the question "Are you going to say it was *her* fault?" is appended only for form's sake, as an after-thought, its implication effectively ruled out not only by the manner in which it is presented but also by Sostrata's inability, born of her innate goodness, to blacken Philumena's name in any way, even in self-defence. For this reason her denial here simply confirms Laches in his attitude, enabling him to reject suggestions that Philumena's absence was either caused by homesickness (235f.) or prolonged by illness (238) in the same way they had been dealt with by Parmeno: as excuses.

240ff.: Laches' tirade ends as it began, with a general condemnation of womenfolk, and mothers-in-law in particular. This time, however, it is a condemnation at variance with information already available to the audience. While responsibility for Pamphilus' marriage, albeit couched in general terms, is here laid at Sostrata's door, it was in fact Laches whom Parmeno earlier made the chief initiating force (116ff.). Laches' outburst has apparently broken free of reality and gives voice to little more than his prejudice - hence the universality of its application.

(II ii-iii)

243-80 Phidippus Laches Sostrata: If the previous scene with its confrontation of Laches and Sostrata was designed to present a tension of uncertainty between the charges of the one and the apparent innocence of the other, the appearance of Phidippus holds out the immediate hope of resolving that uncertainty. In the event, however, Phidippus serves to perpetuate the mystery, partly as a result of the character he possesses, designed to contrast with that of Laches, and partly for dramatic reasons: to heighten suspense by delaying revelation of why Philumena deserted her marital home until this can have its maximum effect - on Pamphilus. This insertion of frustrated expectation and delay indeed may go some way to explaining the iambic septenarii here (see further Introduction: Metre).

Like the earlier appearance of Parmeno, the entry of Phidippus is facilitated by having him address his daughter still inside the house. Similarly, his identity is readily achieved by both his reference to "fatherly affection" (244), and Laches' words at 246ff.

245 not stand in the way: Before ever bringing Phidippus into contact with characters outside his family circle the playwright provides a short objective self-portrait upon which subsequent interaction can be built.

246 just at the right time: The convention of coincidence, common to all drama, by which events, and in particular arrivals, occur when dramatically necessary (Duckworth[2] p.115f.). On occasion such arrivals may be signalled by a character expressing surprise that another is slow to appear (Sophocles' *Oedipus Tyrannos* 73ff., 289, Menander's *Dyskolos* 78ff.). In Roman Comedy in contrast a character will often call express attention to the opportune nature of an arrival, as here.

I'll find out from him: A seemingly illogical statement in view of Parmeno's mention of a meeting between the two old men the day before (191). That it produced no result, however, is made clear by Laches himself at 251. Their dialogue here therefore assumes a quasi-recapitulatory format, portraying Phidippus as a man apparently under the thumb of his womenfolk and hence unable to exercise what both a Greek and Roman audience would feel is his proper authority, ready to acquiesce in his daughter's return and not enquire into its cause until prompted to from outside.

247ff. I know I'm indulgent...: Though Laches' initial address to Phidippus is intended to establish a sympathetic link between them - hence his claim to share Phidippus' indulgent attitude, even if not to the same extent as his neighbour - his general lack of sensitivity reduces the attempt to the level of a crude complaint. That it fails to evince from Phidippus anything stronger than "Is that so?" testifies more to the latter's mildness and the need to avoid open friction at this point, than to Laches' capacity for diplomacy.

253 If we have done anything wrong: Laches' starting point in his attempt to heal the rift between the two families is an implicit acceptance of the *odium* theme as its cause, even if he seeks to disguise the fact by suggesting the onus for continuing the marriage alliance rests with Phidippus (252). To a Greek audience which already knew the truth of the situation Laches' words would have been filled with irony; for a wrong has indeed been done, and Pamphilus has already, if unknowingly, made some amends by marrying the girl (Sewart[1] p.123).

256 because she's ill: It is not fortuitous that Laches refers to the *morbus* theme as a possible explanation in second position. Like Parmeno he places little credence in it as a cause of the present situation and introduces it more as a means of defending his own side, and more specifically himself, against any possible imputation of neglect. To add weight to his argument he is careful to assert his role as surrogate to his absent son, whose love for the girl is forcefully stated and whose adverse reaction to recent events would stem directly from that love and from his position of legal authority over her. Twice earlier Laches introduced the theme of concern for Pamphilus, at 210 & 233. In both cases they served as additional brickbats for use against Sostrata; here Pamphilus is introduced specifically to spur Phidippus into action.

263 Laches...: Phidippus' conciliatory attitude towards his neighbour is highlighted not only by the use of Laches' name but also by the way he accepts and echoes Laches' earlier statements. Thus "care" (*diligentiam*) answers "sufficiently well" (*satis...diligenter*) in 257, while "kindness" (*benignitatem*) echoes the sentiment of "*you* care for her welfare more" (*tu illam salvam...velis*) in 259.

266 if I can possibly bring it about: As 245 indicates, Phidippus really means "but I can't bring it about".

267 complaint against her husband: Since Phidippus' failure to respond positively to the mention of illness disposed of this as the cause of Philumena's recent behaviour, Laches returns to the theme of enmity. Already he has made clear Pamphilus' love for his wife (260), and Phidippus' implicit acceptance of it (264) effectively rules out the young man as the source of marital difficulties, though we might note an element of irony here since Pamphilus' early behaviour towards his wife was aimed at achieving precisely what has happened. Laches' question here, therefore, inviting as it does a negative reply, together with Phidippus' response, now serves to do the same for Philumena - to underline her love for Pamphilus and to reinforce the picture of the loyal wife already established by Parmeno at 164ff. As a result there can be only one alternative explanation for the young couple's problems - Sostrata.

271 There you are, Sostrata: Evident satisfaction on Laches' part at finding his earlier assessment of his wife's culpability borne out by the evidence of others. His observation here is all the more telling since it brings back into dramatic focus a character who since 243 has stood mute on one side, a silent and unmentioned witness to a dialogue which has moved steadily against her. The playwright's neglect of Sostrata till this point in the scene thus becomes not a failure on his part to visualise the stage action, but a device to concentrate attention onto the dialogue of the old men and to highlight Sostrata's helplessness in combating the seeming inevitability of their conclusions.

274ff. Following the departure of Laches and Phidippus, Sostrata's protestations of innocence continue the mystery of conflicting evidence and so help maintain a necessary element of audience sympathy for her. In addition, her speech fulfils the double function of both link and exit monologue, bringing one episode to a close while allowing a smooth transition to the return of Pamphilus (see further Duckworth[2] p.107, Prescott[3&4]).

(III i)

281-335 Pamphilus Parmeno: So far events portrayed onstage have been in many ways recapitulatory, developing themes outlined initially by Parmeno in conversation with Philotis. Only now, with the appearance of Pamphilus himself, is the action set for further revelation and development. As elsewhere Terence introduces his characters as if in mid-conversation, and with Pamphilus already informed of what has happened. In this way the playwright is able to go beyond the simple provision of information and to focus immediate attention upon their respective reactions to the situation, reactions which are themselves founded upon the depiction of a striking contrast. Like Laches before him Pamphilus' opening words set the atmosphere for the whole scene as he launches upon what will develop into a review of his marriage, a review that echoes the details previously given by Parmeno but also inserts the extra dimension of personal crisis and grief. In an effort to balance this the slave attempts to minimise the more serious implications of his master's account, but in the event, when the truth of Philumena's condition becomes apparent, it is Pamphilus' dark assessment that comes closer to the truth, while Parmeno's optimistic platitudes merely signal the end of his pretended role as confidant and the gulf that from now on separates him from actual developments. Through all of this the metres employed by Terence clearly play a role in producing the tempo and emotional tenor of the exchange. Up to 292 alternation of trochaic septenarii and octonarii goes hand in hand with a mood of non-specific disquiet from Pamphilus as he bewails his general lot in life, disquiet countered by Parmeno's relatively specific reassurances. Thereafter the young man's dejected despondency (293ff.), now centred upon more specific detail, is set within the ambit of iambic octonarii (cf. 198ff.), which continue through Parmeno's increasingly irrelevant generalities to the moment of crisis when cries are heard within Phidippus' house.

281 more bitter experiences: Explained in 294-8: first a marriage he did not want, then the loss of Bacchis, now the apparent loss of a wife he had come to love.

126

286f. All of us...pure gain: A sententious, if somewhat ungrammatical finale to Pamphilus' outpouring of emotion, for which Donatus provides the Apollodoran original:

οἱ γὰρ ἀτυχοῦντες τὸν χρόνον κερδαίνομεν
ὅσον ἄν ποτ' ἀγνοῶμεν ἠτυχηκότες.

"those of us in misfortune derive advantage all the time we do not know of our misfortune".

288 But this way...problems: Parmeno attempts to counter his master's despair at returning to find disaster and his resulting attitude of "ignorance is bliss" with his own observation "soonest known, soonest mended". Büchner rightly notes p.130 that one element of the slave's role in this scene is to lighten the atmosphere and thus avoid an aura of total tragedy, as Pamphilus himself recognises in 293.

291 You'll discover...again: The tripartite rhetoric of the line (cf. 65) is designed to bolster Parmeno's optimistic forecast, though in the event it merely emphasises his total underestimation of the situation. Far from resolving the problem Pamphilus' return produces additional crisis.

292 just trifles: cf.781 where Laches' use of the same word suggests his own misunderstanding of the situation and its significance.

293 Why try to comfort me?: Pamphilus' wretchedness here is underlined by repetition of the Latin word *miser* at the end of 293, 296 ("unhappy"), and 300 ("misery").

294 elsewhere: Carney *ad loc.* suggests the vagueness of Pamphilus' reference to Bacchis may stem from a reluctance to equate his earlier love affair with his subsequent marriage, as the use of actual names might do.

296 clear to anyone: cf. Parmeno's observation 128f.

299 What's more...to blame: A telling rejection of Parmeno's even-handed approach to the problem at 290f., which foreshadows subsequent developments as Pamphilus' attempts to defend Philumena by championing his mother inevitably involve an element of blame being attached to the girl, despite all his efforts at damage-limitation (477ff., 485ff.).

301f. Duty calls...something: The dilemma of Pamphilus' position. Recognition of the duty Pamphilus owes his mother (cf. 122) needed no amplification within the text - it was inherent within the moral framework of ancient society. Its inclusion here as a principle the young man accepts at face value and without question does, however, serve a specific function: to mitigate his later specious employment of it as an excuse for not taking his wife back. The debt owed to Philumena on the other hand is now reiterated (cf. 164ff.) not only in order to increase the pathos of the situation envisaged - the apparent loss of such a wife -

but also to help motivate Pamphilus' subsequent willingness to maintain the secrecy of Philumena's disgrace when the easiest course open to him would involve her repudiation. Before the injection of complicating factors which are to cloud Pamphilus' true emotions with varying levels of fabrication and pretence, the playwright seeks to reveal and emphasise the reality of the young man's feelings for both his mother and his wife. The balance of emotion indeed is to some extent underlined by the balanced vocabulary used: the application of *iniurias* 301 ("faults") and 303 ("unkindnesses") to the situation of both women.

306 Good Lord no, a minor matter...: The culmination of Parmeno's attempts to convince his master that the problems he outlined offstage are not serious (cf. 292). Tellingly the reassurances offered are soon to be swept aside by nothing more than noises emanating from inside Phidippus' house.

314 tell them I've arrived: The Roman custom of a husband being announced to his wife after a long absence before actually meeting her.

Hello, what's that?: It is hardly fortuitous or simply the result of the slave being closer by now to Phidippus' house, that Parmeno is made to call attention to the sudden commotion inside. At the very point where the theme of resentment is to be superseded by that centred on illness, the fact that it is Parmeno who initiates the change underlines what the audience soon realises is his total misreading of the situation.

317 You talk away...not to: Parmeno's complaint reinforces again the contrast between himself and his master. Earlier he had made light of the supposed trouble between the two women whereas Pamphilus had more correctly regarded the details given to him as indicative of something serious. Now his preoccupation with himself in the face of clear indications of trouble and his master's growing alarm sets him apart from the real tide of developments.

318 Hush daughter, please: Uncertainty inevitably surrounds the extent to which the Roman audience was able to interpret correctly both the vague noises coming from inside Phidippus' house and Myrrina's actual words. By convention offstage cries by young girls in New Comedy invariably betokened the pangs of labour (Plautus' *Aulularia* 691f., Terence's *The Woman from Andros* 473, *The Brothers* 486f.). The present instance, however, not only lacks the equally conventional appeal to Juno Lucina, goddess of childbirth, but even inverts the convention, since, as Gilula[3] p.145 argues, the clue to correct interpretation of events lies not in the girl's cry itself but in Myrrina's attempt to stifle it. It may well be in fact that with Parmeno onstage precluding any overt pointer to Philumena's true state the playwright has combined theatrical necessity with the dramatically effective maintenance of audience suspense until Pamphilus himself is in a position to break the news. And even if the more perceptive members of the audience were able to see through the present vagueness, their loss of suspense would be more than

128

compensated for by enjoyment of the irony inherent in Pamphilus' assurance to his mother, 354ff., and the playwright's novel variation of the normal convention.

321 I don't know: An effective indication of the growing gulf that separates Parmeno from his earlier role as a source of information. Similarly his weak self-justification "I couldn't tell you everything at once" seeks to cover the fact that he had earlier regarded the idea of illness as a pure fabrication.

325f. Oh Philumena...die with you: Pamphilus' final words before rushing into the house serve as climax to the sense of impending disaster and as confirmation of the genuine feelings of love he has for his wife before the reality of that disaster threatens to drive them irrevocably apart.

327-35 No point...trouble: A link monologue (Prescott[3] p.8) in spoken iambic senarii (indicating a radical reduction in emotion) now serves both as preparation for the entry of Sostrata and as explanation for not following Pamphilus inside; for stay outside they must if any attempt to maintain Philumena's secret is to be made. Parmeno's circumspect attitude to the present situation, however, even with the deterrent of unpleasant consequences for himself should he venture inside (335) seems strangely inappropriate to a slave for whom curiosity is a major characteristic.

328 I can see we're all hated: Despite the emergence of the *morbus* theme into reality as opposed to the excuse that Parmeno earlier believed it to be, the theme of enmity nevertheless continues to dominate his interpretation of the situation and to explain for him Philumena's initial departure from her marital home; hence the prominence he places upon himself in 332 as "a servant of Sostrata's" - Sostrata, who stands at the heart of the enmity and has already been refused entry, cf. 343.

(III ii)

336-60 Sostrata Parmeno Pamphilus: On a purely technical level the entry of Sostrata at this point and her interaction with Parmeno provide the interval of time necessary to cover Pamphilus' discoveries inside (Duckworth[2] p.130ff.). In dramatic terms on the other hand her reappearance at the very moment the *morbus* theme has assumed overriding prominence can only serve as vindication for her earlier protestations and a forceful restatement of her affection for Philumena. This is further reinforced by the shift in metre from Parmeno's earlier spoken iambic senarii to the more 'recitative' style of iambic septenarii. Later, when Pamphilus himself reemerges from Phidippus' house, the juxtaposition of contrasting themes gains additional emphasis: the ostensible cause of the *odium* theme pointedly seeking clarification of her daughter-in-law's illness, a mother welcoming home in relief a son she hopes will resolve the situation at the very point he is to inject a fresh and seemingly devastating level of complication, a questioner seeking information from someone determined not to provide any - as the brevity of his answers makes all too clear.

338 Aesculapius...goddess of health: The god of healing and his attendant deity, Salus.

339 Er, Sostrata!: The continued presence of Parmeno onstage not only enables Sostrata to learn of her son's return before meeting him, but more importantly forestalls what would otherwise have been her natural reaction - to follow him inside. In this way the playwright avoids a problem of his own making: demonstrating her concern while preventing its natural result.

352 How dejected he looks!: Since the possible use of masks in Roman comedy (see above 9 n.) would not have allowed the representation of emotional changes upon an actor's face, and it is questionable whether such changes would be visible to an audience in a large theatre anyway, Pamphilus' state of mind is conveniently established before he comes into contact with the others, cf. 355.

354 She's a little better: A clear attempt at evasion, as Sostrata's subsequent questions indicate. Similarly his reply in 357 "Yes, that's what it was" shows Pamphilus seizing upon the guesses of others as a desperate means to divert attention from the truth, before returning later in the line to further evasion with "So they say". As Büchner observes, p.132, Pamphilus is gradually forced into a corner by his mother's questions (cf. 699ff.); hence his eventual appeal for her to go indoors is little more than a means to escape what is for him an unwelcome inquisition.

357 Nothing serious?: lit. "occurring everyday" i.e. chronic rather than acute.

360 Don't they know...themselves?: The question underlines both the slave's lack of enthusiasm when it comes to work (cf. 443, 814f.), and the fact that Pamphilus' order is inspired primarily to dispense with the danger to the situation Parmeno represents.

(III iii)

361-414 Pamphilus: With Pamphilus' dejected monologue, set in trochaic septenarii, and the revelation of the real reason for Philumena's return to her parents' home the tension built up so far in the action by the parallel development of the *odium* and *morbus* themes undergoes a radical modification. Now at last the audience is able to appreciate something of the dramatic irony that must have existed in the Greek original as it watches the two old men continue to develop the essentially defunct *odium* theme, abetted by Pamphilus himself, for whom it provides a smoke-screen to hide the 'truth'. At the same time, however, we need to bear in mind the degree of irony Terence continues to forego by not revealing the whole truth through an expository prologue (see further 376f. n. below).

361-4 Finding...state: Lines clearly designed to increase expectation through the aura of shock they contain and the vagueness that surrounds them.

365 quite a different ailment: The first hint of a major shift in the *morbus* theme, further heightening the suspense initiated by Pamphilus' vague generalities in reply to his mother's questions.

367 When the maids...: The contrast between Pamphilus' expectations and what he actually discovers is neatly balanced by the reaction of the womenfolk themselves: initial and natural delight at his unforeseen return followed by panic when they realised what it portends. In what follows the playwright continues the theme of contrast by opposing the intentions of the maid who rushes off to warn the others and the result: guiding the young man straight to his wife. This contrasting disparity of intention and achievement is to recur later. Compare for instance the motive which inspires Sostrata's proposal to retire to the country (581ff.) and its significance for Pamphilus, or the expectation of Laches and Phidippus in summoning Bacchis and what it accomplishes in reality.

375 the only cries...dictated: Though Pamphilus' revelations become more and more specific, so that we can hardly doubt the Roman audience would have been aware by now of the narrative's ultimate destination, it is noticeable how Pamphilus is finally able to voice the fact of the pregnancy only by quoting Myrrina's own words. His continuing inability to be totally open creates its own tension for an audience seeking confirmation of its suspicions.

376f. Monstrous...tears: Further contrast of intent and reality: the young husband, full of concern for his wife's well-being, suddenly confronted with what he immediately interprets as her flagrant failure to reciprocate those feelings through faithfulness. As a result, the tears he sheds are those of self-pity, his reaction to the dishonour he believes he has suffered, matched by Myrrina's at 379. At the same time the continuing loss of dramatic irony for the Roman audience when compared to its Greek counterpart is clear: a young man scandalised by a discovery that is of his own making, the description of a mother sinking to her knees before the cause of her daughter's plight, and ultimately in 402 Pamphilus' consent to the possible exposure of his own son.

378f. fell to her knees in tears: As Carney observes *ad loc.*, the pathos of the situation is emphasised not only by the fact that Myrrina debases herself within her own house, where she exercised considerable authority in her own right, but also by the fact that the later scene with Phidippus shows her to be a formidable character, well able to dominate her husband, something already hinted at in 250, 271.

383 She was assaulted by some reprobate: Since it was inconceivable that an otherwise respectable girl would voluntarily enter into an extra-marital relationship (MacDowell p.124, Legrand[1] p.460f.), a pregnancy such as Philumena's could only be represented as the result of rape. That the act took place before her marriage adds a further element of mitigation, maintaining as it does the theme of loyalty to her husband established at 164ff.

385 But when I think...anguish: The insertion of the line serves to separate neatly the factual details of Philumena's state from Myrrina's appeal that it be kept secret, and to mark a shift in Pamphilus' own reaction - from the initial shock of revulsion and self-pity to pity for his wife, born of the love he has for her and which has induced him to accept his mother-in-law's requests.

386 Whatever chance: *fors fortuna*, often personified as a goddess, hence Myrrina's use of it as a means of appeal.

389f. if you have ever...in return: Not a subtle reminder of the debt Pamphilus owes his wife as a result of his unpleasantness in the early days of their marriage - the stress laid upon Philumena's silence in 166 & 302f. effectively rules out Myrrina's knowledge of his behaviour then - nor even a hint at the early non-consummation of the marriage, as has been suggested, but more likely a reference to the couple's happier days before Pamphilus' departure for Imbros, when he was fully aware of his wife's feelings for him.

390 it won't cost you anything: lit. "without effort". In order to ease Pamphilus' acceptance of her appeal Myrrina minimises the implications of compliance. What both quite naturally fail to realise at this point, however, is that the major complications which intervene in the situation will arise not from any reluctance to preserve Philumena's secret on Pamphilus' part, but from the threats to that secret posed by those outside the immediate confines of their conspiracy (see further 409-14 n., 444-50 n.).

391 as for taking her back: Foreshadowing what is to be one of the two major problems faced by Pamphilus in the rest of the play (the other being the existence of the baby). Myrrina's phrasing suggests she leaves open the possibility of the young couple resuming marital relations. To Pamphilus at 403ff. on the other hand the fact that Philumena was not a virgin when she married poses insuperable difficulties for any future together.

393 I'm told: lit. "they say". Myrrina could only have learned of the events she here describes from Philumena, so that the use of the plural verb has usually been interpreted, following Donatus, as an attempt to avoid the embarrassment of anything more specific (contrast, however, Büchner p.135 n.23).

two months...seven months: On the timescale of the pregnancy see Appendix II.

398 I'll say there's been a miscarriage: Implying that the child can be passed off as sickly and disposed of as Myrrina suggests in 400. The exposure or abandonment of infants for reasons of poverty, illegitimacy or simply being the wrong sex (i.e. female) in places where they might be found by others and reared, if they survived at all, thus avoided the stigma of direct infanticide. Its frequency in real life, as opposed to the usefulness of the motif in New Comedy plots, is impossible to gauge (see further Lacey p.164ff., Harrison p.70f., MacDowell p.91, Brothers 615 n.).

400 There'll be no problems for yourself: As in 390 Myrrina now emphasises at the end of her appeal how little she is asking of Pamphilus. Silence on his part protects Philumena's reputation, while exposure of the infant not only removes the evidence of her rape but also frees Pamphilus from the unacceptable prospect of rearing as his own a child that is illegitimate (cf. Fantham p.69). This still, of course, leaves Pamphilus with the problem of explaining his refusal to take Philumena back, as the scene with Laches and Phidippus, 451ff., makes clear. In the event, however, the *quid pro quo* arrangement formulated here is nullified when Phidippus rescues the child from its fate.

402 I gave my promise: The promise and the fact that Pamphilus is prepared to abide by it without question and come what may, are of course essential prerequisites for subsequent action. As a result of it indeed Pamphilus effectively throws away any freedom of action and begins a process by which a trap gradually closes round him (see further 444-50 n.).

405f. life in the future...loneliness: At the end of his account Pamphilus returns to the emotion of 377, self-pity, as he envisages a life without the woman he loves; hence the analogy with his earlier state when forced to give up Bacchis (cf. 294ff.).

409-14 he's the last person...gives birth: While Pamphilus' observation exists specifically to remind the audience that the slave is the only other person with sufficient information to realise the baby cannot have been conceived in wedlock (its essentially functional aspect being underlined by use of the plain iambic senarius metre), the danger this poses has already been prepared for in Philotis' portrayal of him as a character incapable of keeping a secret (110f.). True, the threat posed by Parmeno here is quickly and easily dealt with by sending him off on a wild-goose chase, but its insertion serves as introduction to the more serious difficulties soon to be posed by others, and to bring home to Pamphilus the inaccuracy of Myrrina's earlier assurances. In many ways too the portrayal of Parmeno from this point on constitutes a direct inversion of the normal comic slave-role his earlier self-description suggested: arranging his young master's escape from the problems that beset him.

(III iv)

415-50 Parmeno Sosia Pamphilus: A major function of Parmeno's return onstage and his dialogue with Sosia is to balance the sombre, almost tragic tones of the previous scene with an element of inconsequential humour more usually associated with Plautus (see further Duckworth[2] p.195ff., Prescott[1] p.260f.). Some have suggested indeed that Terence specifically invented the speaking role of Sosia here for this purpose. At the same time the very length of the scene, like the detailed information Parmeno later requires for his mission to the Citadel, increases the tension of the episode in the face of Pamphilus' desperate need to dispense with the slave.

415 an unpleasant experience: For the disagreeable nature of sea travel as a source of humour compare Plautus' *Mostellaria* 431ff., *Trinummus* 820ff.

426f. Well, it...Sosia: Faced with Sosia's earnest description of his perils Parmeno cannot resist the cue for a joke on the runaway tendencies of some slaves, just as his earlier reactions in 418 and 424 "Really?" "Dreadful!" suggest by their brevity that he takes his fellow-slave's agitation less than seriously.

428 But there's Pamphilus: The fact that Pamphilus has been present onstage throughout the dialogue in no way affects the development of the action. Rather, it was a convention of the ancient stage that characters present but not involved in the immediate action simply faded out of attention.

431 It's imperative...Citadel: In Greek terms the Acropolis in Athens. The dialogue here with its initial vagueness is deliberately constructed to maximise Parmeno's feeling of impending work (cf. 360), as he is forced to seek clarification only to his own cost.

433 Myconos: One of the more northerly Cyclades islands. As was the usual practice in ancient Aegean navigation, Pamphilus' vessel evidently avoided crossing open sea as it returned from Imbros to Athens, skirting instead the coast of Asia Minor before heading westwards through the Cyclades.

434f. Damn...safely?: The culmination of Parmeno's sense of unease and suspicion. In antiquity those about to embark on a journey frequently vowed to reward the appropriate god with a gift in return for a safe homecoming. Here, however, the incongruity of the vow Parmeno describes serves both as a source of humour in its own right and to reinforce the earlier picture of him as the disgruntled slave sent to help others with the baggage.

436 What are you hanging around for?: The action has by now reverted to its original aim of sending Parmeno off so that he does not hear Philumena's cries of pain and thus realise the truth of the situation (412ff.). Comparison with 360, however, where there was a similar need to dispense with the slave and the same verb *cessas* was used to hurry him on his way, reveals an altogether different mood. Instead of deep gloom, the humour of the situation continues through the evident lack of purpose in the errand Pamphilus has described so far. Similarly, the repeated insistence on haste in 438 "Now fly!" and 443 "Now run!", constantly frustrated by Parmeno's perfectly reasonable requests for clarification, ensures further highlighting of both Pamphilus' impatience and the air of unreality that surrounds the whole mission.

440f. big chap...corpse: The description is both preposterous and self-contradictory but illustrates well Pamphilus' poor attempts to extemporise.

444-50: A link monologue of reflection and planning which restores the atmosphere of the play to more sombre tones as Pamphilus despairs of being able to keep the promise made to Myrrina. Schadewaldt p.10ff. saw in this an actual shift in Pamphilus' resolve, but as Sewart[1] p.56ff. and Büchner p.140f. argue, it marks instead the beginning of a realisation that his options are narrowing, that the promise so easily given in 402 has become, after its first test, a far more onerous undertaking than first envisaged. By disposing of Parmeno Pamphilus has been able to maintain the promise of silence; the existence of the child and its origins still remain a secret. In the scene that follows, his resolve not to take his wife back is similarly tested. In this respect the reference to duty in 447 becomes an element of foreshadowing for his later development of the *odium* theme; hence the juxtaposition of Pamphilus' pity for Myrrina who here, as it were, represents her daughter, and his debt to Sostrata. This whole section of the play indeed displays clear evidence of careful planning by the playwright as he alternates development of the problems facing Pamphilus, (a) the marriage (b) the child: a) the need to find a reason for not taking Philumena back, 451ff., b) the danger posed by Phidippus' discovery of the baby and his prevention of its being exposed, 516ff., a) Sostrata's removal of her son's excuse for not renewing marital relations, 577ff., b) Laches' acceptance of the child, 650ff., which finally forces Pamphilus into a position where he must choose between the equally disastrous courses of rearing a bastard or revealing his wife's disgrace.

(III v)

451-515 Laches Phidippus Pamphilus: With the reappearance of the two old men the situation from their point of view is returned to the events of 243-73. There Phidippus had revealed Philumena's declared resolve not to return to her marital home while her husband was away. In the context of the audience's present knowledge, of course, her decision was no more than an excuse to cover the pregnancy, an excuse useful at the time but with implications that, like so much else in the play, only become apparent later. In the present scene therefore the return of Pamphilus is naturally interpreted as automatically resolving the difficulties that have so far existed. From the young man's standpoint on the other hand the course of action he has decided upon forces him, after an initial uncertainty in 452f., into resurrecting the *odium* theme in order to maintain the *status quo*. Again, it is a specious excuse he employs, and just as that of Philumena had been negated simply by her husband's return, it is itself destined to be overthrown by the innocent actions of Pamphilus' own mother. As in so many of Terence's dialogues the metre used consists of trochaic septenarii as far as 484, when it converts to iambic senarii.

453 Who's that I hear talking?: Though the more comic forms of aside are generally not overheard, others clearly are and serve as a convenient means of bringing characters into contact, especially when one of them, as here, is less than anxious to converse at all (Duckworth[2] p.112). In contrast, the aside spoken in 454 remains unheard, since it produces no reaction in the others; rather it is designed to remind the audience of Pamphilus' twofold resolve (402f.) before contact proper is established.

458 Well, out with it: The suddenness with which Laches broaches the subject of the inheritance - immediately after meeting his son and with the usual preliminaries of expressing gratitude for a safe return left to Phidippus - both emphasises the brusqueness of his approach, already seen in his treatment of Sostrata, and introduces a mercenary aspect to his character. (On avarice as a besetting sin of old age see *The Brothers* 831ff., Menander's *Aspis* 84ff., Cicero *De Senectute* xviii 65-6, Duckworth[2] p.277f.) Similarly, his reaction at 462 continues in this vein until Pamphilus' pointed observation in 463 causes him to attempt a display of belated regret. Donatus aptly notes on the line that signs of grief only occur once the fact that there is some inheritance is disclosed.

464f. That's a wish...prefer: Commentators are divided on whether this constitutes an aside, designed to indicate the lack of sincerity in Laches' last statement, or whether the final words "and yet...prefer" introduce a sufficient element of sympathy as not to provoke or require a reaction.

466 Yesterday...to his place: As in 458 the suddenness with which Laches changes the subject is hardly accidental. It suggests a determined effort to present an explanation of events before Pamphilus even discovers what has happened. Carney suggests indeed that this anxiety to preempt Pamphilus' discovery of the situation may also lie behind Laches' initial question "Just got back?". The attempt to minimise the girl's absence both in terms of time and cause is of course rich in dramatic irony, made doubly transparent by the blatant methods employed to involve Phidippus in the fiction. Pamphilus' own early intervention with the statement that he knows how things stand (468) serves in fact to underline the flimsiness of Laches' efforts.

466f. Say you gave...Of course: The speed of exchange in these lines with their rapid alternation of both speaker and addressee is itself a considerable source of humour for an audience aware that the old man's efforts are in vain. Similarly, Phidippus' assurance that Philumena will be sent back is a patent and ironic fabrication in view of his admission in 245 & 271 that he cannot control his womenfolk.

468 I know...stand: A line of multiple significance. To Laches and Phidippus it suggests merely that Pamphilus is aware of how long Philumena has been away and the supposed reason for her departure from the marital home: the *odium* theme. Pamphilus himself, however, has progressed beyond this to a potentially far more damaging reality. To an audience that had witnessed an expository prologue on the other hand the claim would become yet another level in the misapprehension that afflicts all those involved in the situation. From this viewpoint the old men's attempts to minimise the significance of events proves ultimately more realistic than Pamphilus' own assessment. At the moment it is they who are working, albeit in ignorance, towards the play's ultimate aim, while Pamphilus is about to introduce further obstacles to his own eventual happiness.

470ff.: Armed with the assurance of his superior knowledge and aware that it has already been used to advantage in scotching Laches' attempted deception, Pamphilus is now able to seize the initiative and to engage in deception of his own based on the theme of enmity revealed to him by Parmeno. At the same time, by an injection of dramatic economy the playwright invites us to assume Pamphilus knows the two old men are themselves aware of the theme and accept it as an explanation for events. That Pamphilus makes no attempt to introduce the theme of illness as explanation here is clearly understandable since 1) it comes too close to the truth he is attempting to conceal, 2) it offers the prospect of the girl's recovery and thus cannot be used as a long-term reason for refusing to take her back, 3) it has been portrayed thus far in Laches' mind as merely an excuse, and so holds no prospect of convincing him that Pamphilus' projected course of action has any justification.

472 faithful, kind and forbearing: An incongruous statement in the light of early relations between the young couple (157ff., 164ff., 302f.), and more appropriate to Philumena than to Pamphilus. While Pamphilus' fidelity may be formally intact in the context of ancient marital expectations, despite his repeated visits to Bacchis (cf. 550-6 n., Plautus' *Mercator* 817ff.), his pretended kindness and forbearance are a self-confessed fiction. Indeed the very moralistic tone he adopts is itself a powerful indication that truth here is in short supply. However, if the *odium* theme is to be reintroduced, the implications of 299 must inevitably intervene, and it is only if Pamphilus' own hands are clean and he is personally free from any feelings of resentment that he can represent himself as the victim of the dilemma he describes at 480 and thus choose on supposedly objective criteria to take a stand on his mother's side.

473 from her own lips: Behind Pamphilus' display of disingenuous modesty is doubtless the realisation that having kept her husband's unkindness secret in the past Philumena now has even less reason to denounce him.

475 who currently does me wrong: By failing to humour Sostrata and leaving her marital home. Compared to the picture of Philumena established so far Pamphilus' stance here can only appear heartless and selfish. In terms of the fiction he is striving to establish, however, it is inevitable. What we need to bear in mind is that the blame implicit in Pamphilus' assertions is itself part of an attempt at damage-limitation designed to avoid the more disastrous disgrace that would result from revelation of the rape (cf. 540), and that Pamphilus himself is soon to offer further mitigation by stressing his continued and genuine love for his wife at 485ff.

476 any fault of mine: The Roman audience remains ignorant of the dramatic irony in the assertion.

478 exercising some self-control: Just as Pamphilus had earlier appropriated to himself qualities to which he had little claim, so he here denies his wife qualities the audience knows full well she exhibited in plenty in the early days of the marriage, albeit in a somewhat different context.

479 no other way: In order to avoid the possibility of Philumena's return at some point in the future being raised, Pamphilus must implant in the minds of the old men the idea that the rift between mother and wife is permanent and thus rules out any hope of reconciliation with Philumena as effectively as the rape does in his own mind cf. 490 n.

481 Under...first: Donatus *ad loc.* comments on the mild terms in which Pamphilus' decision to reject his wife is phrased. Rather than dwelling on Philumena's supposed faults, he stresses the positive aspect of filial duty, an approach calculated to appeal to the older generation. It is worth noting too how the present speech, ostensibly directed towards Phidippus, in fact has its main impact upon Laches, just as that at 485ff., while directed to Laches, is more directly relevant to Phidippus in its reassurances that rejection of his daughter is the result solely of factors beyond Pamphilus' control.

484 feelings of resentment: Precluded from rejecting Pamphilus' decision outright because of its foundation upon duty, Laches is forced into the weaker position of suggesting the young man's alienation from Philumena stems from considerations other than those claimed, i.e. that duty is in fact a pretext. In this he is of course correct, though not as he imagines.

488 I love her and praise her: In view of Pamphilus' earlier reaction to his wife's cries the audience cannot help but recognise the sincerity of his words here. Without it indeed the scene, with its combination of truth and fabrication, loses much of its pathos. By the same token the continuation of his love for Philumena is an essential prerequisite for the ultimate goal of the action. It is not that Pamphilus ever ceased to love his wife, merely that something came between them, something he here chooses to represent in terms of the *odium* theme but which we know is in fact the existence of a seemingly illegitimate child. Büchner p.144 regards Terence's technique here as superior in fact to that possible in the case of an audience which knows the whole truth. For them, he argues, the result of present difficulties would be merely a retardation of the eventual happy ending, not the tension of the Roman play.

490 fate: Introduced like 479 to establish the idea of Pamphilus' helplessness to resolve the situation and the resulting permanence of the rift with Philumena.

493f. It's in your power...come back: Within the space of little more than a line the reactions of the old men effectively overturn the whole of Pamphilus' case. While Phidippus rejects his powerlessness in the face of fate, Laches' low opinion of Sostrata leads him to reject as sheer folly any attempt to champion her in preference to a wife his son claims to love. The result for Pamphilus himself is an impasse from which his only escape lies in flight.

497 didn't I tell you...: Fulfilment of 261f. and ironic insofar as the audience know Pamphilus' actions do not in fact stem from anger at Philumena's return to her parental home. Implicit in the observation is the suggestion of Phidippus' responsibility for the present situation through failing to ensure his daughter's return. To Phidippus on the other hand his daughter's departure from Laches' home was caused by the very absence of Pamphilus (269, 451). The young man's return therefore held out the prospect of a restoration of normality, but by refusing to take his wife back it is Pamphilus in his view who is now acting unreasonably, hence the outburst at 499.

502 give me back her dowry: The sum of money or other property given to the bridegroom by the bride's family upon betrothal did not become his to use as he wished. Rather it marked the bride's contribution to her new family and was held in trust for any offspring of the marriage. In the event of divorce the dowry had to be returned to the wife's father or guardian, a deterrent to any rupture in marital relations without good cause (see further Harrison p.45ff., MacDowell p.87ff., Lacey p.109f.).

506 you've come into a bit of money: Unlike Laches, Phidippus has never been a party to the *odium* theme (cf. 497 n.). Faced therefore with his son-in-law's seemingly unjustifiable behaviour and convinced the breakdown in relations has

only arisen since the return from Imbros, Phidippus seizes upon the one certain
change in the situation, the inheritance, as the cause of present difficulties.

510ff.: Exasperated by his inability to influence either his son or his neighbour,
Laches finds himself abandoned onstage by the very figures whose affairs he has
so far attempted to manage. Unable to vent his sense of frustration on them, he
returns to the one person who cannot walk away from him and whom he continues
to regard as the source of all his problems. Without apparently knowing of
Sostrata's earlier meeting with Pamphilus, he feels certain that the young man's
recent display of perverse loyalty is no less her work. That this is far from the
truth is by now perfectly clear to the audience, but it emphasises the deep-seated
prejudice that forms part of Laches' character. As he disappears inside, his final
word in the Latin, *evomam*, lit. "I shall spew out", sums up through its very
vulgarity the strength and quality of his feelings.

(IV i)

516-76 Myrrina Phidippus: In contrast to the prospect of a repeat confrontation
with Sostrata foreshadowed at the end of the last scene, the sudden appearance
onstage of Myrrina and Phidippus must have created considerable surprise.
Instead of repetition the playwright now introduces a mirror image of 198ff. in
which emphases and events are actually reversed. Thus it is Myrrina, the wife,
who enters first and though her opening words, like those of Laches earlier, set the
immediate emotional atmosphere, her reaction stems from an intimate
understanding of developments, not prejudice as was the case with Laches.
Similarly contrasted is the relationship between husband and wife. The tenor of
Myrrina's initial statements suggests a scene in which she is browbeaten by her
husband, but it is in fact Phidippus who is characteristically forced to give ground
(cf. Wilner[1] p.62). So too in the earlier scene Laches' accusations centred upon
actions of which Sostrata has subsequently been shown to be innocent; here on the
other hand those of Phidippus at times stray perilously close to the truth and it is
only Myrrina's superior knowledge that allows her to deflect him back to
misapprehension with further development of the *odium* theme, this time Myrrina's
supposed dislike of Pamphilus. In terms of metre the dialogue is carried on in
predominantly trochaic rhythms (septenarii and octonarii) followed at 566ff. by
iambic octonarii for Myrrina's closing lament.

519 what reason...a secret: Myrrina's perplexity not only echoes that of
Pamphilus at 444ff. and 450, but also contrasts radically with her assurances at
397ff. Has Terence allowed an element of inconsistency to creep into the play in
order to heighten the tension he wishes to create at the beginning of the scene, or is

he attempting to suggest that Myrrina too now realises her scheme is more difficult to carry through than she once imagined?

521 But there's the door: The sound of the door being opened, caused either by the creaking of the hinges or by the latch being raised, was a conventional means of heralding the appearance of a character from one of the stage houses (see further Duckworth[2] p.116f., Bader).

523 Me, husband?: A telling display of the playwright's insight into the psychology of Myrrina's character: initial panic at the realisation that her efforts to conceal the birth of the child are on the point of collapse, followed by pretended ignorance, first that she has been found out, and second that there is anything amiss. (For pretended ignorance as the conventional response of a guilty conscience compare Pamphilus' reaction to Bacchis' enquiries at 826).

527 Who's the father?: The suddenness of Phidippus' question, the total lack of preparation that marks its intrusion so close to the beginning of the dialogue and the relative ease with which it is rebutted, are powerful indicators that from the old man's standpoint it is more the product of his annoyance than a real suspicion of illegitimacy. Its appropriateness to the situation on the other hand, its very logicality in the face of an unannounced pregnancy when seen from the viewpoint of the audience's superior knowledge, allows the playwright to exploit their awareness of its relevance and to involve them in the shock felt by Myrrina.

Is that a proper question: Myrrina's vehement response forces the milder Phidippus to acknowledge shamefacedly the implications of what he has just suggested, steering him away from the 'truth' through the embarrassment he has brought upon himself. The dramatic irony evident to the Roman audience would have extended further for an audience that had witnessed an expository prologue: to an awareness that what is here foisted onto Phidippus as a lie is in fact the real truth, cf. the old man's belief in 533 that the child will cement the two families together compared to Myrrina's, that it constitutes an obstacle to any future.

531 a normal delivery and at the right time: On the significance of the statement for the chronology of the pregnancy see Appendix II.

532 the death of the child: Once again Phidippus goes to the heart of the situation by his reference to Myrrina's actual intention (400). Ironically, however, the motive attributed to his wife for her 'hypothetical' plan - to weaken the young couple's marriage - is the exact reverse of the truth, an element of misapprehension which offers an escape route into unreality through the further development of enmity.

536 I wish I knew it were so: As unfeeling a response as Laches' earlier outburst against Sostrata (207). Underlying the statement is Phidippus' assumption that Myrrina is lying, that her claim to wretchedness is no more than a front to cover her real contentment at having engineered the break-up of the marriage.

540 Better...the real one: An apt mirror-image of Sostrata's earlier plight. There she had been the helpless victim of Laches' attack, helpless inasmuch as her lack of knowledge prevented her from offering any defence, though certain of her own innocence. Here Myrrina is able to employ her greater knowledge to deflect Phidippus away from the 'truth', and then to acquiesce in the resulting misapprehension, even if this requires that she accepts the role of a 'typical' mother-in-law.

542 I never thought that a vice: See below 550-6 n.

544 you haven't budged an inch: We have no reason to question the correctness of Phidippus' comment here on Myrrina's initial attitude to Pamphilus. What the old man fails to appreciate, however, is the degree to which that attitude has by now changed.

545 undoing the arrangements I made: Essentially the same type of charge as Laches levelled against Sostrata in 242.

550-6: As Donatus points out on 554, Phidippus goes beyond defending Pamphilus' behaviour (542ff.) actually to praise it, an ostensibly radical shift away from his criticism of the young man in 499ff., though motivated in both cases by a desire to counter specific, if differing, threats to the marriage. In the present case he is assisted in developing his argument by the hypothetical nature of the situation he outlines, hence his emphasis upon "Perhaps you heard...". The irony is that the hypothetical visits to Bacchis after Pamphilus' marriage to Philumena do indeed reflect reality. To a modern audience, however, Phidippus' observations, for all the special circumstances that inspired them, cannot help but bring into sharp focus the dichotomy that existed between male and female sexual morality in antiquity. Male society recognised no obligation to restrict a husband's sexual activity to his wife (Harrison p.32). An affair with a *meretrix* did not in effect constitute adultery since it posed no threat to the continuation of the family unit. For a wife on the other hand, whose main function in society was to bear legitimate children, sexual fidelity was an absolute prerequisite.

556-9 Please...daughter: As in 547f. Myrrina makes no attempt to defend herself by denying the role attributed to her, a hazardous venture as she had recognised in 540. Rather, she accepts the premises upon which Phidippus' fabrications are built and uses them to further the establishment of an alternative reality within which Phidippus is steered towards accepting the justice of Myrrina's supposed attitude. Any answer Pamphilus makes to her proposed enquiry will in fact justify her stance: if he is willing to take Philumena back, there is no longer any problem; if he refuses, the attitude attributed to her will be vindicated. Phidippus' response 560ff. shows indeed that he has no answer to the logic of her case; all he can do instead is complain at the lack of consultation. In taking this stance Myrrina must of course rely upon Pamphilus' willingness to maintain his promise, but within the

142

parameters of that promise she shows a considerable lack of concern for her son-in-law - for obvious reasons, since her own daughter's welfare is at stake.

563 I forbid...outside the house: With his will circumvented in the past Phidippus' aim now is to recover control of the situation by blocking any intention Myrrina has to expose the child, an essential move in terms of the play as a whole as the Greek audience was able to appreciate. By ensuring the baby stays where it is, however, Phidippus effectively ruins Myrrina's promise to Pamphilus as part of the price for his silence, plunging both her daughter and herself into an even deeper crisis.

572ff. At the time...his getaway: The presence of these purely factual lines within Myrrina's monologue has often been seen as an element of exposition taken from the prologue of the Greek original and inserted here to foreshadow the dénouement (see Introduction p.11). The mention of a ring for instance, a conventional factor within New Comedy for discovering identities, suggests this may figure in the eventual resolution of the situation. What Terence has omitted at this stage, however, is any reference that would link it to Pamphilus. Instead, by actually reversing the normal convention whereby it is the assailant who loses some article through which he is later identified, the playwright ostensibly rules out what might otherwise have pointed towards escape. As it is, the reference serves instead to emphasise both the violence of the rape itself and Myrrina's own sense of helplessness.

(IV ii)

577-606 Sostrata Pamphilus: Stage action in this scene suggests Terence has been less than precise in accounting for the movement of his characters. References at 358 and 582 ensure consistency as regards Sostrata's presence indoors up to this point, but Pamphilus' departure at 495 and Laches' reaction to it imply he left by one of the wing-exits. Nowhere does Terence explain either how the young man returned home or how he knows nothing of what has gone on inside and has failed to encounter Laches there. By the same token, to hypothesise an entry by the two characters through a wing-entrance may resolve the problem of Pamphilus' movements, but it introduces fresh ones for Sostrata. Rather than total consistency Terence seems instead to present his audience with a piece of action, inviting them to accept its dramatic validity without the necessity of establishing its total logicality. More important for the drama, however, is the relationship between developments here and those in the closing lines of the previous scene: the problems created for Pamphilus by Phidippus now exacerbated by Sostrata's own proposed course of action. Metrically the iambic octonarii that marked Myrrina's monologue are here continued in the dialogue between mother and son.

577 It hasn't escaped me: Though Sostrata initially assumes personal responsibility for the interpretation she outlines here, it soon becomes clear this is not the result of information she has gathered herself. Rather, it is through the intervention of Laches, foreshadowed at 513ff. and specifically mentioned at 582f., that she has come to accept the theme of enmity as the explanation for events. This is not, however, enmity in the active form Laches earlier insisted upon and which he has induced Sostrata to believe is accepted by Pamphilus also (despite the young man's supposed attempts at dissemblance), but rather a passive form, as if there were something inherent and immutable within Sostrata's character to which Philumena took exception. In this way, and only this way, can Sostrata reconcile her own certainty of innocence with the evidence of events, both actual and those represented to her through the distorted interpretations of others. It is only by viewing the *odium* as essentially passive that Sostrata can also be certain in her own mind that the simple act of withdrawing to the country will of itself remove any reason for Philumena not returning. Were the girl's absence the result of resentment at some positive act by her mother-in-law, there could be no guarantee that retirement would actually remove that resentment and so improve the situation.

you've come to suspect: Gilula[3] p.153 aptly points out the pathos of the woman's position here: hurt once by the departure of Philumena and its consequences and now led to believe her own son holds her responsible for the breakdown of the marriage, unaware that Pamphilus knows full well her innocence but cannot admit as much without endangering the edifice of fabrication he has erected.

583 the object of your love: Donatus observes *ad loc.* that the phrase - emphasising as it does the emotional bond between the young couple - holds greater significance than if Sostrata had simply said "your wife". Sostrata's acceptance of this love and hence her appreciation of the sacrifice Pamphilus proposes in giving up his wife thus serve all the better as justification for her own counter-proposal.

584 your feelings of duty: Advanced by Pamphilus at 481 to justify not taking back his wife. Now Sostrata's attempt to reward that duty threatens everything her son tried to achieve there, forcing him into a position where he must reject not only her offer but also, by extension, the duty of obedience to a parent inherent within it (see further Konstan p.137).

587f. no possible reason left...to you: At the very end of her speech Sostrata unwittingly but graphically underlines the danger her proposed course of action contains but in a context that reveals her acting out of the noblest of motives.

589 Give in to her stupidity: As in 470ff., Pamphilus' apparently harsh censure of his wife exists only as an argument in the fictional situation of resentment so far fostered, a small price to pay in return for avoiding the truth. Hence, in order to avoid disaster for Philumena he is again forced into an ever-widening framework of fabrication by representing his mother's offer in the negative light of surrender to petulance, just as in 591 he reinforces the argument with the suggestion that outsiders will see her act not as the unsolicited product of a good nature, but as something forced on her by his obstinacy in refusing to take Philumena back (a charge already levelled against him in 496).

592 public festivals: One of the few occasions in Athenian society in which respectable women were allowed a role beyond the confines of their homes (Lacey p.168).

595-7 anybody...people...Here in town: Though expressed in general terms, Sostrata's desire not to be a burden has relevance only to her immediate family, a further pointer to the pathos of her position, and made all the more powerful by the thought that the only alternative might be expectation of her death.

my advancing years: cf. 231 where Laches used Sostrata's age as a jibe against her.

597 through no fault of my own: An echo of the argument at 580, though as Sostrata realises in 599, the only way of proving she had no ill-will towards her daughter-in-law is in fact to accept the prejudice against herself.

600 common reproach of womankind: That mothers-in-law hate their daughters-in-law, first voiced by Laches in 201, cf. 274ff. By making the end of her speech ostensibly an appeal to self-interest - that her proposed act, though designed principally to benefit Pamphilus, will also help herself - Sostrata effectively renders her son's rejection of the offer all the more difficult, as his reaction in 601 and 605 indicates.

601 this one thing: Deliberately ambiguous. To Sostrata Pamphilus' *cri de coeur*, caught as he is in having to choose between mother and wife, can only refer to the *odium* theme that has ostensibly imposed the dilemma upon him. To the audience on the other hand the "one thing" that has come between the young man and his wife is the rape.

606 Me too: After the quasi-positive light in which Sostrata has represented her retirement to the country this becomes a gentle reminder to both Pamphilus and the audience of the real suffering the present situation has caused her, not least, we may note, from the husband who now joins the conversation.

(IV iii)

607-22 Laches Sostrata Pamphilus: Terence makes no attempt to indicate within the text at what precise moment Laches emerged from his house and appeared onstage - whether he was in fact visible to the audience before his first statement -

or why. Dramatically on the other hand his intervention serves to reinforce the difficulties Sostrata has created for her son by underpinning the offer of retirement with the authority of a husband's command (610) and removing from Pamphilus any further opportunity to deflect his mother from her intended course of action. The rapid interchange of dialogue and the tension of the scene are well represented by the mingling of long trochaic and iambic metrical forms throughout.

607 my dear: lit. "wife", in stark contrast to the brutal "woman" of 214, though Laches' ingrained antipathy towards his wife soon resurfaces in the curt instructions he gives her and the peremptory finale "That's all I have to say", in the Latin the single word *dixi*.

611 That's very much my hope: Though spoken in response to the prospect of no more than mutual toleration, this for Sostrata is far better than the recriminations to which she has recently been subjected.

614 I'm still undecided...wife.: Not true from the audience's viewpoint, as Pamphilus' earlier statements and his aside at 616 make clear, but part of the stance he has assumed within the ambit of the *odium* theme.

615f. That's really...resolve: An important aside designed to provide a pointer to the true state of Pamphilus' feelings in the midst of a situation clouded by misapprehension and excuses, designed also to emphasise that the obstacle to a resumption of marital relations is moral and social, not emotional, cf. 488 n.

617 I think...take her back: A textually disputed line, but in essence Pamphilus attempts to establish in a positive light his continuing refusal to take Philumena back. Other editors (Dziatzko, Stella, Carney) prefer to read "I don't think...if I take her back". While detailed interpretation of Pamphilus' statement may vary, its significance lies in the desperation that marks its introduction and the ease with which Laches is able to sweep it aside. His belief that Sostrata's retirement will of itself allow the return of Philumena, and that the attitude of the two women towards one another is in consequence unimportant so long as they are kept apart, effectively undermines any continued resistance by Pamphilus. At the same time, however, Laches' response underlines his preoccupation with the semblance of family harmony rather than its reality, cf. 218.

621 The Old Couple: The exact significance of the reference is unknown, but Laches probably attempts to use against his son the same appeal to pathos and self-pity he earlier directed against his wife, 223ff.

(IV iv)

623-726 Phidippus Laches Pamphilus: The entry of Phidippus, motivated like 243ff. by his annoyance with Philumena, mirrors the earlier scene between the young man and his mother in the complications it produces for Pamphilus. There Sostrata's generous offer had struck at her son's resolve not to take his wife back; here Phidippus initiates a similar assault upon his unwillingness to accept the child, forcing him ever deeper into that corner from which ostensibly the only escape lies in revealing the truth about Philumena's pregnancy. Increasing the pressure upon the young man and further emphasising his plight is Laches' own reaction to his son's continued resistance. From the dismissal of arguments in the previous scene he now turns to accusations, in some respects taking over the mantle of Phidippus himself at 499ff., while at the same time putting the final seal on a predicament initiated for Pamphilus by his own mother. Throughout, the scene is constructed in iambic senarii, the metre of plain spoken dialogue.

623 I'm angry with you too, Philumena: A reminder of Phidippus' earlier altercation with Myrrina, which for a moment raises the prospect of involving Philumena herself in yet another variation of the already complex web of family dissension, before Phidippus diverts attention back to Myrrina as the supposedly real source of responsibility.

628 How shall I explain it?: i.e. Pamphilus' continuing refusal to take his wife back.

629-32 Tell...situation: The lines neatly encapsulate how ready both old men are to blame their wives for the situation.

633 That's quite an about-turn!: The aside is clearly designed to show Pamphilus' surprise at developments since he was last in contact with Phidippus, when the burden of blame rested on Sostrata. Like his next aside (634) it serves in fact to keep the audience informed of the young man's thought processes as he gratefully seizes upon anything that allows a continuation along his chosen avenue of fabrication and excuse. In addition, the air of flippancy which typifies these comments contrasts strongly with the storm to come.

635-8 My own...child: Lines constructed to produce the maximum of effect. First, there is the contrast between Phidippus' long-held desire that the marriage-tie continue (despite his outburst at 499ff.) and what he regards as Pamphilus' own ambivalence in the matter; hence the emphatic *ego* in the Latin: "I for my part (wish)" i.e. "my own wish" at the very beginning of his statement followed by the scarcely veiled reference to marital separation in "If, however, it turns out you have other ideas". Then there is the deliberate delay in referring to the child until the very last word, a device much used by Plautus for comic effect (Duckworth[2] p.356ff.), but here introduced to maximise the shock felt by Pamphilus and allow a contrast with Laches' own reaction. So far Pamphilus' silence as regards the rape has been founded on the assumption that the threat posed by the child will be circumvented through its concealment and subsequent exposure. Though the possibility of the child's existence becoming more widely known was recognised as early as 397, this in itself was never seen as posing a threat to the understanding reached, since there was still the possibility of claiming the baby had miscarried. In his final words, however, *accipias puerum* "take the child", Phidippus introduces not only that widening of knowledge, but worse still, the suggestion that its supposed father accept responsibility for its being reared, since in the event of divorce it was the father who gained automatic custody of any offspring.

639 We've got ourselves a grandson: Phidippus' phrasing emphasises the positive link between the two families the baby represents.

643ff. But what kind...as being: Despite his happiness Laches typically cannot resist the opportunity to criticise, just as he earlier did at 247ff.

648f. If I had...with her: After the momentary vacillation of 615f. caused by conflicting claims of emotion and propriety, a conflict first recognised in 403ff., Pamphilus' aside underlines the even greater need to follow the latter now that the complicating factor of the child's status has been brought into the open. The position of the aside, immediately before Laches' assault upon the last vestiges of Pamphilus' earlier excuses, is of course hardly accidental.

652 a son to call you father: The focus of the whole play's potential tragedy. Despite this the audience cannot have been unaware of the humour that exists in the stark contrast between 'reality' and the optimism shown by the old men, their belief that all problems are now resolved.

655-60: Following the collapse of the *odium* theme as thus far developed Pamphilus attempts one final variation by suggesting that the secrecy of the birth indicates Philumena's dislike for him. In this he relies upon the intimate link between the girl and baby already established in Laches' mind (as shown by his last two statements) to avoid the real danger at hand: forced acceptance of the child. Rejection of the baby alone after all can only be based upon its illegitimacy. The weakness of his case, however, is evident even before Laches' rebuttal: 1) Philumena's own stated reason for leaving her marital home in 269 was precisely the absence of Pamphilus, not his presence - to the audience a specious excuse but one never disproven in the eyes of Laches or Phidippus; 2) responsibility for causing the present situation lies with Myrrina not her daughter, a theme introduced by Phidippus at the beginning of the scene and now employed by Laches as a weapon against his son. Ironically too, though it was Laches himself who gave Pamphilus the cue for this latest theme by his disapproval of the pregnacy's secrecy in 645, it is also Laches who now rejects the validity of similar disapproval when voiced by Pamphilus (Gilula[3] p.155).

664-8 You two...child?: Like Laches at 510ff. Phidippus reacts with exasperation to a situation seemingly taken out of his hands. Significantly, however, his annoyance now serves to sunder the very link that Pamphilus has striven to preserve - between Philumena and the child - hoping that by rejecting the one he can avoid the danger posed by the other. By abandoning any interest in the future of the marriage Phidippus unknowingly brings about a concentration of attention onto the ultimate crisis, and as in 638 it is the final word he utters that bears the full weight of that crisis. To make matters worse, the fact that it is Laches who responds effectively removes from Pamphilus any further say in the future of the child, presenting him with a *fait accompli* he knows to be an abomination.

670f. When its own...bring it up?: Pamphilus' question, like that of Phidippus in 527, takes the situation to the brink of tragedy. As Laches' response indicates, he has heard something of the aside, but how much? Commentators have often been troubled by the possibility of only partial overhearing and have resorted to textual emendation or reinterpretation to allow the whole to be heard. Their efforts, however, have invariably foundered on either the unnecessary nature of proposed changes or the contorted reasoning introduced. The form of Laches' reaction, "What, not bring it up...", clearly suggests only partial understanding, that the extent of his hearing is limited in fact to the two last words, *ego alam*, "should I bring it up?", tellingly placed at the beginning of 671.

673 I really can't...any longer!: With Pamphilus' rejection of the child the theme of emotional entanglement takes a new turn. By now earlier explanations of the situation, based on enmity, have either been proven incorrect or have faded into insignificance before the implications of the birth. Even Pamphilus' attempt to shift the burden of responsibility for marital breakdown onto Philumena herself pales before a child regarded as providing proof of a physical link between the two families, a child Pamphilus knows, however, effectively destroys that link. To Laches on the other hand his son's rejection of the infant marks a rejection of the very basis of family life; hence for an explanation he is forced to go beyond the family and return to the love-affair with Bacchis with which the play began.

675 those tears of yours: When and how has Laches become aware of them? Unless the reference is to Pamphilus' behaviour when forced to marry or his outbursts at 651 and 653, the only tears seen by others onstage are those mentioned in 355, the basis perhaps of Donatus' explanation "It appears that Laches has heard about this from Sostrata, for he himself has not come upon his son weeping".

684 After all the time...affair: Laches' description of his earlier patience is somewhat at odds with the account given by Parmeno in 115ff., a discrepancy doubtless caused by the change in the source of information and the differing aims.

689 you've given your heart back: A further example of Laches' tendency to alter and even invent facts to fit his interpretation of events. There is for instance no suggestion that he is here referring to his son's continued visits to Bacchis after the wedding or even knows of them, and clearly since his return from Imbros Pamphilus has had no opportunity to resume relations with his former mistress.

Rather, the accusation marks a desperate attempt to account for Pamphilus' recent behaviour by making his earlier resistance to the prospect of marriage applicable to present circumstances. (On the illogicality of Laches' arguments in this speech see Sewart[3] p.255f.)

690 in complying with her wishes: The verbal echo of the Latin *obsecutus* here and in 688 strengthens the contrast between earlier ostensibly correct behaviour and what Laches now sees as a lack of moral fibre in his son - his assumption that it is Bacchis who constitutes the dominant force in the affair. From this in turn stems Phidippus' belief that termination of the affair can be achieved by an approach to Bacchis.

694 live with that woman: The climax in a series of ever more serious accusations against Pamphilus: 1) that he has become emotionally attached to Bacchis again, 2) he has fallen under her spell, reverted to his old way of life, and thereby wronged his wife, 3) he is now attempting to render the relationship permanent by forcing a rupture with Philumena and replacing her with Bacchis. As an indicator of their displeasure neither Laches here nor Phidippus in 716 refers to the woman specifically by name.

695 What other reason: In the full flood of his anger Laches either forgets Philumena's reported reason for leaving her marital home (269) or regards it as no more than an excuse, as indeed it was.

698 or tell us why you can't: Forced by circumstances into a corner and having just denied that continuing relations with Bacchis lie behind his refusal to take Philumena back, the only reason that Pamphilus is now in any position to offer is the truth, effectively ruled out by its results for the girl herself, the promise made to Myrrina, and by the very presence onstage of Phidippus (cf. Menander *Samia* 488ff. where Moschion finds himself in the same predicament).

699 Then take the child: A restatement of the division that has existed in the theme of Philumena's and the child's futures since 664ff. Laches here unwittingly forces his son into an even more difficult situation by treating separately what Pamphilus knows is essentially the same problem. Ironically his observation in 700 "*It* certainly isn't to blame" is the exact reverse of reality.

701-5 I'm completely...in this: The longest aside in the play and important dramatically since it marks the young man's last statement before control of events is finally taken over by others and a resolution of the play's problem effected. After a restatement of the impasse Laches has placed him in Pamphilus once again resorts to escape from the scene as the only course open to him. Just as his departure at 495 was motivated by a desire not to lose control of the situation and to prevent Laches from undermining his resolve to side with his mother, escape here is seen as one last means of defending the decision not to accept the child since in Attic law it was only the father who determined whether an infant be admitted to membership of the family. By extension too escape also signals Pamphilus' determination to keep his promise to Myrrina by not revealing the truth and thus to continue protecting Philumena.

711 She told me so herself: No less than Laches earlier, Phidippus here displays a considerable facility for altering facts to suit circumstances. But for 537-9, a reference to events that occurred before the play began, Myrrina has expressed no opposition to Pamphilus as her son-in-law beyond acquiescing in a role Phidippus forced upon her. Free, however, from the need to apologise for his womenfolk, and a witness to Laches' outburst against his son, who is here revealed as the 'true' guilty party, Phidippus now feels able to convert what was once a reproach against his wife into an instance of perceptive insight and to use it at 712: "I didn't like to tell you..." in much the same way as Laches' jibe at 497.

714 he's totally set against married life: The positioning of Phidippus' final point is significant, emphasising as it does the gulf that separates the old man from reality. The audience knows full well the true extent of Pamphilus' love for his wife.

715 What advice can you give?: Further evidence of the change in relationship between Laches and Phidippus. So far it has been Laches who has been the dominant personality and the source of advice: 249, 497. Faced now with apparently incontrovertible evidence (much of it of his own making) that his son lies at the root of current difficulties, faced too with the realisation that the confidence he once placed in his ability to manage the situation has led nowhere, he is forced to seek advice from the very character he earlier deemed unable to control affairs.

719 Boy!: Used to summon from indoors a slave, who must appear, cross to Bacchis' house, enter, deliver his message, and presumably return before 727.

725 do you want me around?: Since a three-way conversation might easily lead to a diminution of dramatic tension and Phidippus' understandably hostile attitude to Bacchis offers little prospect of a successful encounter, he is sent off, leaving the more powerful personality of Laches to put the other's plan into operation.

(V i)

727-67 Bacchis Laches: Bacchis emerges from her house conventionally accompanied by two maids, referred to in 773 & 793 (cf. *The Self-Tormentor* 245ff., *The Eunuch* 506, 581, Prescott[2] p.111f.). At first both she and Laches are preoccupied with establishing their emotional attitudes to the coming encounter through initial asides set in iambic octonarii. Thereafter, when contact is established, their concern lies in reaching mutually recognised positions that will allow a more meaningful exchange of views (predominantly iambic septenarii).

Then, when Laches finally attempts to put into action his plan of warning off Bacchis (alternating long iambic and trochaic rhythms), her response at 750ff. wins an easy acceptance from him - in many respects too easy, since he never subsequently pursues the question of what really lies behind Pamphilus' resolve once he is persuaded an affair with Bacchis is not the cause (see further 753 n.). Instead he is diverted into the process of using Bacchis to convince Myrrina of this fact, from which in turn springs the dénouement.

728 I've a pretty good idea...wants: It is now several months since Bacchis has had any contact with Pamphilus. Her understanding of the situation therefore can extend only to the fact that something to do with Pamphilus must lie behind Laches' summons. By giving the impression of greater knowledge, however, Terence is able to inject additional tension from the outset.

735 the reputation...my actual conduct: The essence of the dichotomy in the portrayal of Bacchis (cf. 159 n.). The frank recognition here of the opprobrium that surrounds her profession and the confidence she has in the correctness of her behaviour now begin the process of reversing earlier impressions of her as the typical grasping *meretrix* (cf. 756ff., 773ff., 788f.).

737f. I can't expect...indiscretions: Just as Bacchis has been careful to stress that she is not the *meretrix* of common imagination, so Laches is at pains to underline the propriety of his own position. In his case, however, it is a propriety born from a sense of moral superiority and intended to instil in her a due regard for his position and parental authority. Thus his reluctance to offer an insult where undeserved is founded on a belief that he is dealing with a social inferior, but the irony of his belief becomes clearer as Bacchis' innate goodness comes to the fore, just as Laches' attitude that compliance with his wishes will bring advantage to Bacchis (764ff., 792, 794ff.) contrasts with her own self-motivated desire to do what she can for Pamphilus (758ff., 774ff.).

741f. For that...use to me: Spoken with a tone of curt irony which in effect rejects the position of inferiority Laches has sought to establish for her.

743 But what's this all about?: Bacchis' enquiry brings to an end the initial bout of shadow-boxing. Laches now abandons the careful circumspection of his previous approach and presents his complaint "You're receiving visits..." not as a suggestion or hearsay but as a blunt statement of fact reinforced by his insistence that he be heard out, despite Bacchis' attempts to intervene. In this way, Büchner argues p.157, he aims to make evasion of the charge impossible.

746f. so while...as you now are: Donatus observes *ad loc.* the skill with which Laches presents as advice what is in fact a warning.

748 Who's making this claim?: As in 741f., Bacchis studiously avoids being drawn into responding to Laches' insults by trading like for like.

His mother-in-law: But for the reported reaction of Myrrina in 709ff. the real source of the accusation is Laches himself. His reply, therefore, can be interpreted either as a further instance of his ability to transfer facts, or as indicative of a desire to maintain a quasi-neutral stance as "adviser" by shifting responsibility onto others.

752 I have kept...he got married: Only now is the negative picture of Bacchis established by Parmeno at 158f. shown to be little more than a subjective and inaccurate interpretation of events. That his analysis was indeed inaccurate is clear from the absence of any subsequent developments to counter the impression given here. Rather than the typical *meretrix* we now begin to see a woman who once pointedly sacrificed her own interests in order to strengthen her former lover's marriage and is soon to risk hostility and insult in an effort to reunite the young couple.

753 That's very good of you...you did: By this stage Laches has clearly abandoned his initial intention of warning off Bacchis, and he seeks instead to enlist her help. This rapid and fundamental change in his approach suggests in fact that he has come to accept any premise, any explanation, if the results which follow from it hold out the prospect of a solution.

759 the last people: A telling indictment of Laches' recent behaviour especially in view of the fact that the "false rumour", centred upon a supposed renewal of relations with Bacchis, originated with Laches himself and was only later given ostensible confirmation by Phidippus.

760 he deserves...I can give him: From the audience's point of view Bacchis' offer to help her former lover is filled with near tragic irony; for being based upon a false premise - Myrrina's supposed belief in a continuation of the affair - it holds out no hope of an end to the real problem, which remains firmly the question of the child's true parentage. Rather than a resolution, therefore, Bacchis' intervention threatens the one last alternative to the truth (cf. Büchner p.159).

762 it was mine too: Only when he has induced Bacchis to go along with his proposal does Laches widen responsibility for the false rumour to himself, its real source.

765ff.: At what is apparently the end of his interview Laches returns to the attitude he had at its beginning: the head of a household dealing with an outsider - one who may not now pose a threat, but who still needs to be controlled.

(V ii)

767-98 Phidippus Laches Bacchis: Despite the danger of repetition caused by the reappearance of Phidippus at this point and his involvement in a situation already developed by the other two, despite too his earlier reluctance to be present while

Bacchis was onstage, it is of course essential that he be drawn into the arrangements made by Laches, not least so that at the end of the play he can be left in the same state of ignorance as Laches himself. Metrically the scene is built upon iambic septenarii.

769 But when...and drink: The introduction of the Nurse not only provides an economic pretext for the reentry of Phidippus after his departure at 726, but also allows a brief interlude of mild humour with a passing hint at the conventional alcoholic tendencies of such characters (cf. *The Woman from Andros* 228ff., Wilner[2] p.270).

771 Bacchis here swears solemnly: Though Laches attempts to bring Phidippus into contact with Bacchis (while averting the old man's predictably hostile reaction to her through an immediate assurance of her innocence), Phidippus' response underlines the contrast between the standpoints of the two old men: to Laches Bacchis is merely his son's former mistress; to Phidippus she is still the seducer of his daughter's husband. As a result Bacchis herself is forced to intervene in order to soothe Phidippus' annoyance by a personal declaration of intent which repeats her earlier declarations of sincerity.

773 Here are...method of torture you like: The offer is prompted by what underlies Phidippus' barbed repost: the assumption that people like Bacchis are beyond the reach of either scruple or principle. In consequence any oath they might give is totally without value. Both Attic and Roman law held in fact that the truth of a slave's testimony could only be guaranteed if made under torture, hence the reference to it here. By the same token a refusal to allow one's slaves to be subjected to legal torture constituted a *prima facie* admission of guilt (Harrison p.170, MacDowell p.245ff.).

775f. If I succeed...avoid: In essence a repetition of 756, but now used in the context of Phidippus.

779ff. If your wife...if my son...his resentment: The twin cornerstones of Laches' interpretation. The first, and in his view the real source of contention - centred as it is upon Myrrina's supposed opposition to the marriage - he envisages as solved by the intervention of Bacchis; the second he here converts into pique that might delay but cannot prevent a reconciliation. In a quite unjustified display of optimism therefore Laches foresees a solution from two directions, suggesting as a consequence its inevitability.

that's a mere trifle: Laches' evaluation of the birth, the real source of difficulties in this play, indicates graphically how wide a gulf separates his understanding from that of Pamphilus and the audience.

785 It's only *their* minds: Though Phidippus' reluctance to question Bacchis stems technically from the playwright's desire to avoid unnecessary repetition, it does also underline a tendency in his character to accept situations as they are and not to press his own viewpoint too vigorously (243ff., 271, 541ff., 635ff., 664ff., 722, cf. Sewart[1] p.180). By the same token his acquiescence in the course of action the others have devised signals his acceptance of Bacchis' assurances as regards the affair, while allowing him to continue avoiding direct contact with her.

791: MSS other than A insert the line "PHIDIPPUS: I promise they'll be friendly to you when they understand the situation." either after 783, where it makes no sense, or at 791 after "LACHES: ...why you've come", where it virtually repeats the old man's statement. This, plus the fact that the sentiment it contains is quite out of keeping with the thinly veiled hostility Phidippus has displayed towards Bacchis in the rest of the scene, leads editors to regard it as spurious and therefore to omit it.

794-8: An exit monologue designed, like the entrance monologue which follows, to occupy the time that Bacchis is indoors. From the audience's viewpoint Laches' forecast of the thanks she will earn seems decidedly ill-founded. In the event, however, it proves perfectly valid, though not for the reason Laches imagines.

(V iii)

799-880 Parmeno Bacchis Pamphilus: The scenes that take the play to its conclusion now form the three stages by which the dénouement is brought before the audience: first, the suggestion that something momentous has happened and that the ring, mentioned by Myrrina at 574, lies at the heart of the matter. To the more astute members of the audience the details given in 811f. would doubtless have been sufficient to explain in full the resolution of the plot. The degree of separation between the two references to the ring on the other hand and the apparent irrelevance of the earlier instance within the conventional context of lost rings in New Comedy (see 572ff. n.) ensure the need for the second stage: the detailed exposition by Bacchis in a monologue of what her discoveries signify. Finally, with the entry of Pamphilus himself the audience is presented with the outcome of the previous monologue in tangible form, leading in turn to decisions being made concerning the level of understanding other characters are to be allowed. By this means the playwright effectively dispenses with the need for any further involvement on their part, enabling the play to come to its natural end. Metrically the episodes alternate between trochaic septenarii (Parmeno/Bacchis, 799-815), iambic septenarii (Bacchis, 816-40), and finally a mixture of long trochaic and iambic lines for the encounter of Pamphilus with his former mistress.

800 all day: In this way Parmeno is made to emphasise the extent of his exclusion from events, even if his reference to "all day" is something of an exaggeration.

803ff. Please sir...Pamphilus?: Given the negative reply to the first question the rest are patently otiose, but indicate, like the direct form in which the report is given, Parmeno's weary desperation to find Callidemides, his readiness to approach the enquiry from every angle possible.

805 I don't think...exists: Parmeno is correct, but what he does not know, and never will, is why. The theme of his ignorance, which forms a prominent element of humour in these closing sections of the play, is emphasised in the present scene by the frequency of his enquiries beginning in 806 - a total of seven questions between here and his departure at 815 - and by Bacchis' pointed observation in 810 "Don't ask questions when it's none of your business." (cf. Pamphilus' "No, I won't." at 874).

816-40: Technically a link monologue, which Prescott[3] p.120f. likens to that from Pamphilus at 361ff. insofar as it covers the absence of a character for a much longer period than is usual with this device. Further similarities are remarked upon by Gilula[3] p.156: 1) both are delivered by characters who emerge from Phidippus' house and relate events that took place inside involving Myrrina, 2) the former establishes the problem caused by the rape, the second resolves it.

818ff. I'm giving him back...suspicions: Before explaining how revelation of the truth has been effected Bacchis first repeats the problems that have faced Pamphilus since his return from Imbros.

822 about ten months ago: Reckoning by lunar months = nine calendar months.

just after dark: Terence nowhere feels it necessary to explain how a respectable young girl like Philumena happened to be out of doors unaccompanied after dark. Elsewhere in New Comedy such rapes are usually set at night-time festivals (Menander's *Epitrepontes* 473ff., *Samia* 38ff.) where a girl might easily become separated from her companions. Terence's failure to provide more information, therefore, may indicate his reliance upon the convention to avoid lengthy treatment (cf. Terence's *The Brothers* 469f.). Alternatively a detailed exposition may well have been thought inappropriate at what is essentially the dénouement, the very point when Pamphilus is at last able to redeem in full his earlier wrong.

826 He pretended he hadn't heard me: Clear evidence of a guilty conscience, cf. 523 n.

829 he'd pulled...in the struggle: A slight discrepancy with Myrrina's account at 574, where the theft of the ring occurred as the assailant made his getaway. If the change is indeed deliberate, its cause may be Terence's attempt to imply here that the theft was merely an accidental concomitant to the rape.

837-40 While circumstances...he causes: A direct contradiction of the impression given earlier by Parmeno that the affair ended on less than amicable terms. This in turn prepares for the atmosphere of continued mutual respect when Bacchis and Pamphilus are eventually brought into contact.

(V iv)

841ff.: Pamphilus' delight upon his reentry, together with the repetition of Bacchis' message in 845-7, indicate he has already grasped the full significance of what has been discovered, thereby obviating the need for further explanation by Bacchis in front of Parmeno. That Pamphilus should nevertheless be hesitant to accept in full what he has been told is aptly noted by Donatus *ad loc.* "What we most desire we are the slower to believe has been achieved".

850 Nothing of course: Like the laborious confirmation of detail that precedes, Parmeno's disgruntled reaction to his master's gratitude injects an element of humour which complements the evident sense of relief produced by the dialogue. From this point on Parmeno is once again shouldered out of the action and pointedly kept in ignorance of developments, an ignorance which significantly he himself now admits.

856 my own dear Bacchis: Just as Bacchis' own attitude to her former affair was established in 837ff., so here Pamphilus' first statement serves to set the emotional tone of genuine gratitude upon which their ensuing exchange is founded.

864 very much a lady: The Latin *perliberalis* echoes Parmeno's own description of Philumena in 164: *liberali...ingenio* " a respectable character".

865 her father: Though the Latin does not specify whose father is meant here, the obvious inference for the audience is that it refers to Phidippus, from whose house Bacchis has recently emerged. Interpretation as Laches on the other hand remains possible from Pamphilus' standpoint, since in the young man's mind it is his own father who has come to represent the main source of his problems. It may well be in fact that the ambiguity is deliberate.

865ff. No need to...everything: Ostensible refutation of typical comic technique, allowing the playwright to introduce a more naturalistic ending. While, however, restriction of the truth in the case of Laches and Phidippus avoids the need for repeated scenes of revelation or the discomfiture of the old men such as happens to Smikrines in Menander's *Epitrepontes* (something inappropriate to the serious tone of *The Mother-in-Law*), the total neglect of Sostrata in the closing scenes is less well justified, as is Pamphilus' failure to gain self-knowledge from the discoveries made, and hence his failure to gain also our total sympathy (cf. Goldberg p.152, 166, Introduction p.14f.).

869 Yes...kept: The ease with which Phidippus will believe Myrrina's assurances is also guaranteed by his willingness all along to accept a restoration of the marriage (263ff., 635ff., 722ff., 783).

872 as we want it: At this point, with the difficulties upon which the play was founded now resolved, Bacchis probably withdrew into her house leaving the stage ready for a finale of quiet humour as Parmeno makes one last, but inevitably unsuccessful, attempt to penetrate the veil of ignorance imposed upon him. Failing to get at the truth by means of a direct question in 873, he resorts to bluff (874 & 877) but at every turn finds his efforts parried and blocked.

875 I brought...how?: Editors are divided as to whether Parmeno's words here are to be taken as a question or as a puzzled statement, "I somehow (brought) him back from Hell, dead as he was...". In either case the slave is interrupted before he can finish since Pamphilus intervenes before the verb "brought" can be introduced in the Latin.

876 how much you've done for me: Ironic in reference to a character who has been so reluctant to carry out the instructions given to him.

880 Give your applause: A formal request for applause, marking the end of the play in a theatre which had no curtain, is found in this or a slightly longer form ("Farewell and give us your applause") in all of Terence's plays. The MSS mark the appeal with the Greek letter omega, interpreted by Bentley (n. on *Andria* 981) as a textual corruption for CANTOR on the basis of Horace's *De Arte Poetica* 154f.: "If an appreciative audience is what you want, one that waits for the curtain [of the later Roman theatres] and will sit till the singer (*cantor*) says 'Give your applause'...". The correctness of such an interpretation, however, or assignment to a 'reciter' (*recitator*) whom some MSS of the 5th century commentator Eugraphius claim spoke the words, is open to serious doubt. It is clear for instance that in most Plautine plays similar, if more fulsome, appeals were delivered either by the whole cast or by one of the actors, a practice mirroring that found in the closing lines of Menander's plays where these are still extant *(Dyskolos* 965ff., *Samia* 733ff., *Misoumenos* 464ff.). In view of this it seems otiose to introduce an otherwise unheralded intrusion at the end of *The Mother-in-Law* when Parmeno, either alone or in concert with Pamphilus, could easily pronounce the appeal.

Appendix I

The *Odium-Morbus* Theme

While the action of *The Mother-in-Law* is based upon the relatively simple facts of Philumena's departure from her marital home and Pamphilus' refusal to take her back because of what he finds on his return from Imbros, the actual complications within the play stem largely from attempts either to explain the situation and through explanation to effect a resolution, or to prevent the revelation of factors that can only prove disastrous to those at the centre of events. In pursuit of both aims characters have recourse to two recurrent themes which serve at times as either the key to understanding or excuses designed specifically to prevent any meaningful understanding: the themes of *odium*, enmity or hatred, and *morbus*, illness.

Of the two, that of *odium* clearly undergoes the more detailed, varied and wide-ranging development, involving in turn all the central female characters and eventually even Pamphilus himself. Moreover, the actual representation of it within the play at times goes through radical alteration depending on whether it is portrayed in its full emotional intensity, or whether for immediate contextual reasons it is softened into the cognate realm of *ira*, anger or resentment, as at 289, 291, 305, 307, 313, 351, 711. The shift, as Sewart[1] p.154f. observes, usually takes place when a character wishes to refer to the theme without giving offence to another, or hopes to mitigate its seriousness.

The *morbus* theme in turn has its own element of complexity, since the illness referred to by Parmeno in 188 and later by Laches at 239 is viewed by them as no more than an excuse, and therefore remains distinct from what is discovered by Pamphilus on his return. Hence, at no time is this later affliction offered as a valid explanation for Sostrata being barred from Phidippus' house: the motive for that continues to be centred upon *odium* (328ff., 342ff.).

The first mention of the *odium* theme itself comes from Parmeno in conversation with Philotis at 179ff., and while the implication of his words is to place the onus of responsibility upon Philumena, there is as yet no suggestion that its cause lies in any act or attitude on the part of Sostrata. Within ten lines comes the first mention of the illness, 188, a balance of form only, however, since it is clear that the slave regards it as no more than a pretext for not admitting his mistress to see her daughter-in-law.

On the entry of Laches at 198 an immediate and important shift in the theme of *odium* overlays the earlier use of it by Parmeno with the old man's jaundiced view of his wife and his desire to rescue the young couple's marriage, a marriage he had himself arranged. The result is the abandonment of the slave's quasi-neutral depiction of the rift between Sostrata and Philumena with the suggestion that something must actually have caused the girl's dislike of her mother-in-law, and since Philumena herself must remain beyond reproach, that cause must lie with Sostrata (231ff.). In this way two comic conventions are brought together: first, the biased prejudice of an old man against his wife, second, the reputation of mothers-in-law in popular mythology and most comic genres (cf. 201, 277f.). Thus Laches is able, without any real information, to reject both explanations for recent events offered by Sostrata in 235f. and 238, while by the same token Sostrata's own innate goodness effectively prevents her from advancing any defence of herself that might reflect upon Philumena. Though certain she has done nothing to deserve the girl's dislike (228, cf. 276), Sostrata is clearly incapable of attempting to rescue her own reputation by shifting blame onto the girl, a factor which in Laches' eyes is tantamount to an admission of guilt. Indeed it is clear from the manner in which Sostrata couches her only explanation for Philumena's departure, 235f., that she really has no credible solution to offer at all. Here too, then, we see a balance in form, if not in the vigour with which the two themes are presented, between *odium*, advanced as the cause of the situation by Laches, to whom any suggestion of illness is a fabrication, and *morbus*, advanced by Sostrata to explain Philumena's continued absence, if not her actual departure, and to whom the use of enmity as a charge against her seems totally undeserved.

The entry of Phidippus, the girl's father, offers an immediate prospect of clarification. Indeed it is in an effort to achieve this that Laches is so specific in the suggestions he offers for Philumena's continued absence, 252ff., though we may note that his inclusion of illness here seems more a formality, born of a desire to cover all eventualities, rather than indicative of his acceptance of it as a possible reality. In the event, however, the very vagueness of Phidippus' statements, especially in referring to "whims" (245) and in reporting Philumena's own stated reason for leaving (269), serves merely to confirm Laches in his view and to prevent any advance in understanding beyond surmise and theory. With the return of Pamphilus himself on the other hand the audience is presented with the 'truth' at last. Before this, however, the young man becomes involved in a resumé of what is already common knowledge: 1) the estrangement of the two women, though this time expressed in the milder term of *ira* or resentment, 2) the responsibility of one or other of the women for the situation (299), and 3) the theme of *morbus*, as Philumena's cries are heard within Phidippus' house (316ff.). The fact that the slave had singularly failed to make any mention of illness to his young master in the dialogue leading up to the cries (322) underlines indeed the way he continues to see it - as an irrelevance; for while Parmeno is now obliged to accept the reality of an illness, he persists in his inability to connect present reality with earlier references to it (cf. 328ff., 342ff.). If anything indeed he now sees an extension of *odium* to include the whole of Laches' household. To Sostrata in contrast, when she reappears following Pamphilus' dash inside, the cries must constitute a confirmation of what she has long believed.

The manner of Pamphilus' reemergence from Phidippus' house, his appearance, the grudging vagueness of the replies given to Sostrata's enquiries and his evident desire to clear the stage of other characters, all prepare the audience for the shock to come. In his monologue the erstwhile validity of the *odium* theme is completely undermined with the announcement of the pregnancy, a development not altogether unforeshadowed if the audience was able to connect the noises offstage with the conventional cries by young girls in New Comedy (Plautus' *Aulularia* 691f., Terence's *The Woman from Andros* 473, *The Brothers* 486f. Sewart[1] p.124f. suggests similar potential foreshadowing of pregnancy in the references to illness at 330, 334, 337, 356f.). While revelation of the pregnancy ends the reality of the *odium* theme as an explanation, the problems that now face Pamphilus cause him to resurrect it, this time as an excuse for not taking Philumena back. Almost immediately, however, the negative implications of Pamphilus' course make themselves apparent with the return onstage of Laches and Phidippus; for within the context of the supposed dissension between Sostrata and Philumena the young man's decision to take his mother's part carries with it the inescapable reverse conclusion that it is his wife who is to blame for the situation (474ff.). From the point of view of ultimate damage limitation on the other hand, it seems a preferable course to the revelation of the disastrous truth (cf. Myrrina's statement at 540). Pamphilus' aim here and in successive scenes in fact is to accept the misapprehension discovered on his return, together with its source in the theme of *odium*, and to develop its consequences in a tone of high morality in order to produce the result both he and Myrrina have agreed upon. At the same time the undoubtedly genuine love Pamphilus has for his wife leads him to attempt a restriction of the *odium* theme solely to the Sostrata-Philumena axis, to deny any involvement in it for himself or any suggestion that his wife is acting against him (485ff.). By these means Pamphilus poses as the (willing) victim of circumstances not of his making, a victim reluctantly forced to take sides but personally untouched by the enmity involved and thus able to maintain a neutral stance in his emotional relationship to both mother and wife. It is, we have to admit, a stance wide open to counter-argument, as Laches' reaction suggests, hence the need for a speedy exit from the scene at 495.

While Laches' reaction to his son's attitude portends further accusations against Sostrata (513ff.), events onstage undergo a radical change with Phidippus' discovery of the baby and the resultant shift of the *odium* theme to a Myrrina-Pamphilus axis. Ostensibly the old man's charges against his wife augur a repetition of the earlier Laches-Sostrata confrontation. Differences in their respective personalities, however, combined with Myrrina's superior knowledge, ensure her ability to place responsibility onto her son-in-law in an effort to protect Philumena at all costs, and to see him blamed (556ff.) despite the evident obligation she is under as a result of their pact of silence. The danger presented to that pact by Myrrina's attitude is, however, short lived; for almost immediately it is overshadowed by Phidippus' determination to ensure the infant's survival (563ff.) which has its own, far more serious, implications (575f.).

At this point in the action the stance so far adopted by Pamphilus - of refusing to take his wife back and of siding with his mother - comes under successive attack from two directions. First, Sostrata's offer to retire to the country undermines the theme of filial duty, which stemmed from Pamphilus' reaction to the supposed *odium* between his mother and wife and with which he hoped to cloud the issue of resuming marital relations. Once Sostrata, the ostensible cause of enmity, is out of the way the very proximity of the two women to one another (cf. 181ff.), will be removed and with it in Laches' view the *odium* itself. In making her offer Sostrata does not of course signal her acceptance of the *odium* theme in its totality; there is no real inconsistency between her position here and earlier views. Rather, for the sake of her son's happiness she is now prepared to sacrifice both her own analysis of events and her future presence in town. The furthest she actually goes towards recognition of *odium* as a cause is to admit that some unwitting act on her part may have been a source of friction (580). To Pamphilus his mother's offer returns the situation to a choice between revelation of Philumena's disgrace in an effort to prevent resumption of marital relations or acceptance of a sullied marriage and rearing a bastard child as his own - disastrous in either case; hence the force of his resistance, even to the point of further criticism levelled against his wife (589, cf. the belated attempt at mitigation 601f.). The second attack on Pamphilus' position comes with the reintroduction of Phidippus, bringing with him not only a further widening of the knowledge that a baby exists, but also a final end to the Sostrata-Philumena axis of the *odium* theme through the blame now attached to Myrrina. Together they not only remove any possibility of Pamphilus maintaining even a vestige of his earlier ploy, but also confirm the need for a resumption of marital relations because of the physical link between husband and wife that the baby constitutes. The desperate nature of Pamphilus' position now comes to the fore in the very means by which he seeks to avoid the choice before him - his shift of the *odium* theme to a new Philumena-Pamphilus axis, a theme introduced as a possibility as early as 267 only to be immediately dismissed. That this latest strand of enmity, however, is but a variation on that already attached to Myrrina is clear from Laches' reaction in 660ff. To make matters worse, following his exasperation at 664ff. Phidippus effectively separates the two factors that have so far been inextricably bound together in Pamphilus' mind: relations with Philumena and the baby. It is the prospect of losing a wife while yet being forced to accept an illegitimate child that leads in 671ff. to the final variation as Laches reverses responsibility for the *odium* theme and sees as its root cause his son's desire to resume the old affair with Bacchis. Much in the old man's arguments is of course illogical, an illogicality which exists not simply to allow the introduction of Bacchis, as some have argued, but to underline the extent of Laches' misapprehension before the first stages of dénouement. That Phidippus too becomes drawn into this prepares for their joint disappearance from the action and the ease with which they are eventually allowed to remain ignorant of the truth, convinced as they will be that the whole *odium* theme was no more than an enormous misunderstanding, which is indeed the case, though in a far different sense from what they supposed.

Appendix II

The Timescale of the Pregnancy

During the course of *The Mother-in-Law* a number of characters (Pamphilus, Myrrina, Phidippus and Bacchis) all make statements germane to the timescale of events involved in the action - from the initial rape to the actual birth of the child. At two points, however, the information given appears to preclude consistency in the timing of the pregnancy, and commentators remain divided in their attempts to resolve the issue.

The actual references to the timescale are as follows:

376f. Pamphilus. I took one look, burst out with "Monstrous outrage!" and immediately dashed off in tears...

392-4. Myrrina. No one else but you knows that she's in labour and that you're not the father: I'm told it was two months before she slept with you, and it's now seven months since she came to you.

397-9. Myrrina. But if we can't avoid them finding out about it, I'll say there's been a miscarriage. I'm certain no one will suspect otherwise; no one but will think the child is really yours, which is how it seems.

409-13. Pamphilus. Here's Parmeno with the slaves: he's the last person who needs to be involved in this. He's the only one I confided in at the time that I didn't touch my wife when we were first married. If he hears her repeated cries, I'm afraid he'll realise she's in labour. (cf. 136ff.)

527-31. Phidippus. Our daughter has had a baby. Well? Nothing to say? Who's the father?

    Myrrina. Is that a proper question for her father to ask? Good grief! Who on earth do you think but the husband she was married to?

    Phidippus. I suppose so. It hardly becomes a father to think otherwise. But I'm at a loss to know the reason you were so anxious to hide this birth from us all, especially when it was a normal delivery and at the right time.

822f. Bacchis. I remember how about ten months ago he came rushing in to me just after dark...

    The problem of consistency lies essentially in any attempt to reconcile Phidippus' acceptance that the birth of the child was "at the right time", 531, with Myrrina's apparent statement, 392-4, that the young couple have been married for only seven months, and the significance of Pamphilus' reaction upon seeing his wife in labour, 376: that the child could not possibly be his.

    Of the two approaches to the problem offered in the past the first, put forward by Hildebrandt p.29ff., and more recently supported by Kuiper p.41f. n.3 and Carney p.146f., suggests the following scheme:

Rape:	10 (lunar) months
Marriage:	9 months
Consummation:	7 months
Departure for Imbros:	5 months

On this time-scale the pretence of a full-term pregnancy within marriage becomes distinctly feasible, thus justifying Phidippus' claim that the birth came "at the right time", and explaining - if this is indeed necessary - why Laches makes no comment on the timing of the birth when he learns of it. By the same token, however, it blatantly contradicts the most obvious interpretation of Myrrina's statement in 392-4 and seriously weakens the force of Pamphilus' reaction to the sight of Philumena in labour, since there would be no reason for him immediately to reject a 7-month foetus, which was regarded as viable in terms of both ancient medicine and law, as Donatus at 531 recognised (cf. Schadewaldt p.3 n.2, Sewart[1] p.224f.). In order to overcome these difficulties commentators have had recourse either to reinterpretation of 393-4 or to rejection of the lines as spurious on the grounds that they interrupt the flow of sense from 392 to 395 (see further Büchner p.135). While, however, such a course removes the problem caused by references to two and seven months, its extreme nature cannot but imply an element of desperation and should only be admitted if all else fails.

One further obstacle to Hildebrandt's scheme exists in the treatment of Parmeno within the rest of the play. At 409-14 Pamphilus realises that the slave knows too much of events in the early months of the marriage and that by implication a live birth will represent to him, as it does to Pamphilus, the illegitimacy of the baby. Such a conclusion, however, could only be valid in terms of a live birth after a supposed five-month gestation period; in the context of 7 months gestation a live birth is merely premature, not impossible. Carney's objection, that Parmeno will learn of the child at some stage or other anyway, so rendering the whole elaborate arrangement to maintain his ignorance ultimately futile, is based upon events that lie outside the scope of the play and is therefore irrelevant to the action seen onstage.

The second scheme, based on Donatus' note on 393, the confused text of which is discussed by Martin[1] and Sewart[1] p.221f., is best exemplified by Schadewaldt p.2ff., supported by Bianco[2] p.103f., Mras p.193f., and Sewart[1] p.219ff.:

Rape:	9/10 months
Marriage:	7 months
Consummation:	5 months
Departure for Imbros:	3 months

Comparing this with the more obvious interpretation of the information provided by the text, we cannot fail to be impressed by the level of agreement between the two; for it explains 1) the force and immediacy of Pamphilus' reaction, 2) the reason why Myrrina believes she can pass off the birth as a miscarriage if necessary (398) and 3) the need to remove Parmeno from the scene. Only Phidippus' description of the birth as "at the right time", together with the failure of Laches to use the supposedly premature birth as a possible reason for explaining Pamphilus' refusal to take his wife back, constitute obstacles to unqualified acceptance. In the case of Phidippus' belief that the birth occurred "at the right time", the observation of Donatus at 531, that seven-month foetuses were recognised as viable, has led some wrongly to suppose that Phidippus equates such a gestation period with a full-term pregnancy. This is clearly not so, even allowing for the vagueness of ancient authorities as to the correct length of gestation (Censorinus, *De Die Natali* VII 5 records periods between 7 and 11 months being recognised as full-term); for while a seven-month foetus may be recognised as possible, this cannot mean it is the <u>same</u> as a full gestation period.

Acceptance of Schadewaldt's scheme must therefore admit the inconsistency of 531 as a weakness in the playwright's structuring of the time-scale involved, or find some dramatic reason to explain it that does not founder on the rock of special-pleading. At 527 Phidippus blunders unknowingly onto the supposed truth of the situation with his question "Who's the father?", momentarily bringing the play close to tragedy, so close indeed that the theme of illegitimacy is never again introduced by either old man to explain Pamphilus' behaviour. The introduction of such a suggestion by Laches for instance would require a direct denial by means of a lie and the development of a whole new avenue of dramatic potential. As it is, both Laches and Phidippus are simply allowed to remain in the grip of their self-generated misapprehensions to the end. That Phidippus' question does, however, substantially threaten the very comic nature of the play is shown by the vehemence of Myrrina's response, which leaves Phidippus accepting somewhat shamefacedly the impropriety of his suggestion, and it may well be that his assertion of the correct timing of the birth is an indication not so much of his statement's accuracy as of his embarrassed attempt to backtrack on his question and thereby to make amends.

On another level the whole dispute concerning the time-scale of the pregnancy rests upon an implicit assumption that the drama <u>must</u> be self-consistent in every respect. This, however, is hardly a prerequisite for theatre on any level, the plots of which are often founded upon an implausible set of premises in the first place. In producing *The Mother-in-Law* the playwright was clearly faced with two basic requirements in the presentation of the situation: 1) Pamphilus' realisation that he cannot be the child's father, 2) acceptance by the two old men that the child is *prima facie* legitimate (for them to admit the theme of illegitimacy at any length would have resulted in quite a different play). Within these two parameters the possibility of development is naturally restricted. Pamphilus' reaction at 376 requires the marriage to have taken place no less than seven months previously in order to ensure the appearance of minimum viability for any foetus, and no more than nine months, to avoid coincidence with the rape. If therefore, in his efforts to maximise the tension of his stage reality the playwright emphasises the former in order to heighten the pathos of Pamphilus' position, and at other times allows the implication of a normal pregnancy so as to avoid the old men introducing the unwanted theme of illegitimacy as more than a fleeting possibility, if he goes beyond the logic of the real world to achieve his dramatic ends, are we really to complain?

Short Bibliography

Amerasinghe C.W. The Part of the Slave in Terence's Drama, *Greece & Rome* 19, 1950 p.62-72.

Arnott W.G (1) *Menander, Plautus, Terence*, Greece & Rome New Surveys in the Classics 9, 1975.

Arnott W.G (2) *Menander*, London 1979.

Ashmore S.G. *The Comedies of Terence*, New York 1908.

Austin J.C. *The Significant Name in Terence*, Univ. of Illinois Studies in Language and Literature 7, Urbana 1923.

Bader E. The Ψόφος of the House Door in Greek New Comedy, *Antichthon* 5, 1971 p.35-48.

Beare W. (1) Masks on the Roman Stage, *Classical Quarterly* 33, 1939 p.139-46 = *The Roman Stage* App. I.

Beare W. (2) *The Roman Stage*, 3rd ed. London 1964.

Beare W. (3) The Secret of Terence, *Hermathena* 56, 1940 p.21-39.

Bianco O. (1) La cronologia delle commedie di Terenzio, *Annali della Scuola Normale Superiore di Pisa* 25, 1956 p.173-90.

Bianco O. (2) *Terenzio: Problemi e aspetti dell' originalità*, Rome 1962.

Bieber M. *The History of the Greek and Roman Theater*, 2nd ed. Princeton 1961.

Blum R. Studi Terenziani II: Didascalia e prologhi, *Studi Italiani di Filologia Classica* 13, 1936 p.106-16.

Brothers A.J. *Terence, The Self-Tormentor*, Warminster 1988.

Büchner, K. *Das Theater des Terenz*, Heidelberg 1974.

Carney T.F. *P. Terenti Afri* Hecyra, Salisbury, Rhodesia 1963.

CHCL = *The Cambridge History of Classical Literature*, vol II ed. E.J. Kenney & W.V.Clausen, Cambridge 1982.

Clifford H.R. Dramatic Technique and the Originality of Terence, *Classical Journal* 26, 1930-1 p.605-18.

Denzler B. *Der Monolog bei Terenz*, Zurich 1968.

Donatus, *(Aeli Donati Commentum Terenti)* ed. P. Wessner, Leipzig 1902-5.

Duckworth G.E. (1) The Dramatic Function of the *servus currens* in Roman Comedy, in *Classical Studies Presented to Edward Capps*, Princeton 1936 p.93-102.

Duckworth G.E. (2) *The Nature of Roman Comedy*, Princeton 1952.

Eugraphius, ed. P.Wessner (*Aeli Donati Commentum Terenti* vol. III) Leipzig 1908.

Fantham E. Sex, Status, and Survival in Hellenistic Athens: A Study of Women in New Comedy, *Phoenix* 29, 1975 p.44-74.

Fields D.E. *The Technique of Exposition in Roman Comedy*, Chicago 1938.

167

Flickinger R.C. (1)   A Study of Terence's Prologues, *Philological Quarterly*, 6, 1927 p.235-69.

Flickinger R.C. (2)   On the Originality of Terence, *Philological Quarterly* 7, 1928 p.97-114.

Flickinger R.C. (3)   Terence and Menander, *Classical Journal* 26, 1931 p.676-94.

Frank T.   Terence's Contribution to Plot Construction, *American Journal of Philology* 49, 1928 p.309-22.

Garton C.   *Personal Aspects of the Roman Theatre*, Toronto 1972.

Gelhaus H.   *Die Prologe des Terenz*, Heidelberg 1972.

Gestri L. (1)   Studi Terenziani I: La cronologia, *Studi Italiani di Filologia Classica* 13, 1936 p.61-105.

Gestri L. (2)   Terentiana, *Studi Italiani di Filologia Classica*, 20, 1943 p.3-58.

Gilula D. (1)   Where Did the Audience Go?, *Scripta Classica Israelica* 4, 1978 p.45-9.

Gilula D. (2)   Exit Motivations and Actual Exits in Terence, *American Journal of Philology* 100, 1979 p.519-30.

Gilula D. (3)   Terence's *Hecyra*: A Delicate Balance of Suspense and Dramatic Irony, *Scripta Classica Israelica* 5, 1979-80 p.137-57.

Gilula D. (4)   The Concept of the *Bona Meretrix*: A Study of Terence's Courtesans, *Rivista di Filologia e di Istruzione Classica* 108, 1980 p.142-65.

Gilula D. (5)   Who's Afraid of Rope-Walkers and Gladiators?, *Athenaeum* 59, 1981 p.29-37.

Goldberg S.M.   *Understanding Terence*, Princeton 1986.

Gow A.S.F.   On the Use of Masks in Roman Comedy, *Journal of Roman Studies* 2, 1912 p.65-77.

Grant J.N.   *Studies in the Textual Tradition of Terence*, Toronto 1986.

Gratwick A.S.   *Terence, The Brothers*, Warminster 1987.

Grimal P.   L' ennemi de Térence, Luscius de Lanuvium, *Comptes Rendus de l'Académie des Inscriptions et Belles Lettres*, 1970 p.281-8.

Handley E.W.   *The Dyskolos of Menander*, London 1965.

Harrison A.R.W.   *The Law of Athens: The Family and Property*, Oxford 1968.

Henry G.K.G.   The Characters of Terence, *Studies in Philology North Carolina* 12, 1915 p.57-98.

Hildebrandt F.   *De Hecyrae Terentianae Origine*, diss. Halis Saxonum 1884.

Hunter R.L. (1)   The Comic Chorus in the Fourth Century, *Zeitschrift für Papyrologie und Epigrafik* 36, 1979 p.23-38.

Hunter R.L. (2)   *The New Comedy of Greece and Rome*, Cambridge 1985.

Jachmann G.   P. Terentius Afer, *RE* Stuttgart 1934 II, 5, 1 p.598-650.

Konstan D.   *Roman Comedy*, Ithaca 1983.

168

Kraus W.   *Ad Spectatores* in der römischen Komödie, *Wiener Studien* 52, 1934 p.66-83.

Kuiper W.E.J.   *Two Comedies by Apollodorus of Carystus, Terence's* Hecyra *and* Phormio, Mnemosyne Suppl. 1, Leiden 1938.

Lacey W.K.   *The Family in Classical Greece*, London 1968.

Ladewig J.   Beitraege zur Kritik des Terenz, Prog. Neu-Strelitz 1858.

Lafaye G.   Le modèle de Térence dans l'*Hécyre*, *Revue de Philologie* 40, 1916 p.18-32.

Legrand P.E. (1)   *The Greek New Comedy*, trans. Loeb, New York 1917.

Legrand P.E. (2)   A propos du dénouement de l' "Hécyre", *Revue des Etudes Anciennes* 43, 1941 p. 49-55.

Lefèvre E.   *Die Expositionstechnik in den Komödien des Terenz*, Darmstadt 1969.

Lindsay W.M. (1)   Plautina, *Classical Review* 19, 1905 p.109-11.

Lindsay W.M. (2)   Pugilum Gloria (Ter. *Hec.* 33), *Classical Quarterly* 25, 1931 p.144-5.

Lindsay W.M.& Kauer R.   *P. Terenti Afri Comoediae*, 2nd ed. Oxford 1958.

Lowe J.C.B.   Terentian Originality in the *Phormio* and *Hecyra*, *Hermes* 111, 1983 p. 431-52.

MacDowell D.M.,   *The Law in Classical Athens*, London 1978.

Marouzeau J. (1)   Pour mieux comprendre les textes latines, *Revue de Philologie* 45, 1921 p.149-93.

Marouzeau J. (2)   *Térence*, Paris 1942-9.

Marti H. (1)   *Untersuchungen zur dramatischen Technik bei Plautus und Terenz*, Winterhur 1959

Marti H. (2)   Terenz 1909-59, *Lustrum* 6, 1961 p.114-238; 8, 1963 p.5-101, 244-64.

Martin R.H. (1)   Donatus on *Hecyra* 393, *Bulletin of the Institute of Classical Studies* 19, 1972 p.113-6.

Martin R.H. (2)   *Terence* Adelphoe, Cambridge 1976.

Mattingly H.   The Terentian *Didascaliae*, *Athenaeum* 37, 1959 p.148-73.

McGarrity T. (1)   *Thematic Analyses of the Plays of Terence*, diss. Columbia 1977.

McGarrity T. (2)   Reputation v. Reality in Terence's *Hecyra*, *Classical Journal* 76, 1980-1 p.149-56.

Mras M.K.   Apollodorus von Karystos als Neuerer, *Anzeiger den Ost. Akad. Wiss. Wien* 85, 1948 p.184-203.

Norwood G.   *The Art of Terence*, Oxford 1923.

OCD = *Oxford Classical Dictionary*, 2nd ed., ed. N.G.L.Hammond & H.H.Scullard, Oxford 1970.

Palmer L.R.   *The Latin Language*, London 1961.

Posani M.R. (1)   Originalità artistica dell' "Hecyra" di Terenzio, *Atene e Roma* 42, 1940 p.225-46.

Posani M.R. (2)   Sui rapporti tra l' "Hecyra" di Terenzio e l' *EKYPA* di Apollodoro di Carysto, *Atene e Roma* 44, 1942 p.141-52.

Prescott H.W. (1)   Inorganic Roles in Roman Comedy, *Classical Philology* 15, 1920 p.245-81.

Prescott H.W. (2)   Silent Roles in Roman Comedy, *Classical Philology* 31, 1936 p.97-119; 32, 1937 p.193-209.

Prescott H.W. (3)   Link Monologues in Roman Comedy, *Classical Philology* 34, 1939 p.1-23, 116-26.

Prescott H.W. (4)   Exit Monologues in Roman Comedy, *Classical Philology* 37, 1942 p.1-21.

Raven D.S. *Latin Metre, an Introduction*, London 1965.

Rees K.   The Three Actor Rule in Menander, *Classical Philology* 5, 1910 p.291-302.

Sandbach (1) =   Gomme A.W. & Sandbach F.H.   *Menander, A Commentary*, Oxford 1973.

Sandbach F.H. (2)   *The Comic Theatre of Greece & Rome*, London 1977.

Sandbach F.H. (3)   How Terence's *Hecyra* Failed, *Classical Quarterly* 32, 1982 p.134-5.

Sargeaunt J. *Terence*, Harvard & London 1912.

Schadewaldt W.   Bemerkungen zur *Hecyra* des Terenz, *Hermes* 66, 1931 p.1-29.

Segal E.   *Roman Laughter: The Comedy of Plautus*, Harvard 1968.

Sewart D. (1)   *The "Hecyra" of Terence in Relation to its Greek Original*, diss. Leeds 1971.

Sewart D. (2)   A Note on Terence *Hecyra* 670, *Classical Philology* 68, 1973 p.215-7.

Sewart D. (3)   Exposition in the *Hekyra* of Apollodorus, *Hermes* 102, 1974 p.247-60.

Shipp G.P. *P. Terenti Afri* Andria, 2nd ed. Oxford 1960.

Stavenhagen K.   Menanders *Epitrepontes* und Apollodorus *Hekyra*, *Hermes* 45, 1910 p.564-82.

Stella S. *P. Terenzio Afro* Hecyra, Milan 1972.

Warmington E.H. *Remains of Old Latin*, London 1935-40.

Weber E. *Die* Hecyra *des Terenz*, diss. Wien 1940.

Webster T.B.L. *Studies in Later Greek Comedy*, 2nd ed. Manchester 1970.

Wessner P. *Aeli Donati Commentum Terenti*, Leipzig 1902-5.

Willcock M.M. *Plautus,* Pseudolus, Bristol 1987.

Wilner O.L. (1)   Contrast and Repetition as Devices in the Technique of Character Portrayal in Roman Comedy, *Classical Philology* 25, 1930 p.56-71.

170

Wilner O.L. (2) The Character Treatment of Inorganic Roles in Roman Comedy, *Classical Philology* 26, 1931 p.264-83.

Wright J. *Dancing in Chains: the Stylistic Unity of the Comoedia Palliata*, Papers and Monographs of the American Academy in Rome 25, Rome 1974.